No Rich, No Poor

No Rich,
No Poor

Why a failed economy must give way
to a program of common prosperity

CHARLES ANDREWS

Needle Press

ISBN-13: 978-0-9679905-3-8 (acid-free paper)
ISBN-10: 0-9679905-3-X (acid-free paper)
Needle Press / Oakland, California

Library of Congress Control Number: 2009928325

CONTENTS

Preface

The economic collapse of 2008 was a disaster for millions of people. They were laid off work. Homes were foreclosed, and families evicted. People lost their health plan and worried how they could add prescription costs to a shrinking monthly budget. Children were put into larger classes. People at or near retirement age woke to find that a chunk of their so-called investments had disappeared.

During the boom years common people had no seat at the banquet table. It is true that some of the rich, if they missed grabbing a fistful of bailout money, now have to write smaller numbers for their wealth, but they still enjoy their luxuries while anxiety stalks the land.

This book is about more than a boom and bust. The economy over the last 35 years has dealt most people a harsher life than the generation of their parents experienced. Analysis of this failure shows that after the country somehow gets through the current depression, mass prosperity will not return.

Protest against an endless stream of deprivations is inevitable. Movements will arise in forms that we have never seen before. Fundamental changes are coming in the political and economic institutions that set the terms of our work, our standard of life, our personal projects and dreams.

When? We cannot predict the timing, but we can determine what must be done. The existing economic order has reached its limits. It must give way to a new commonwealth founded on principles of prosperity for all. It is in the interest of 90 percent of the population, and it can be achieved. A society of no rich and no poor is no longer a dream. There is no other way to put an end to the economic catastrophes and social antagonisms that are upon us.

Before 2008, there had not been a major depression for over 50 years. The only economic system on a worldwide scale was capitalism, which all authorities declared eternal and unchallengeable. However, the fairly widespread prosperity of the decades after World War Two was disintegrating. The situation of common people was getting worse not better. It is like drips from the ceiling every time it rains. During a break in the weather you get out a ladder and climb up to the roof. You see that patches here and there will not stop the rot. We need a new roof.

Once we see where things are going and why, we can set our bearings on a program worth fighting for. We can get to a better life sooner. That is the aim of this book.

Thirty-five years of decline

For almost a hundred years before 1973 millions of people won a better life in the United States. They had work, they could see they were building a prosperous country, and by fighting many tough battles they won a share of the fruits of their labor and inventiveness. Prosperity was not universal, but it was real.

The year 1973 turned out to be a turning point. Since then life has been getting harder for common people.

It used to be that more than half of employed men in their working prime, age 40 to 44, had been at their job ten years or more. Today, only one-third of these men have the same job security.[1]

Do working people hold their jobs for shorter periods because they are moving to better positions – or because employers toss them out more often? Declining income gives the answer. Men working full-time year-round in 2007 earn less, in inflation-adjusted dollars, than men earned in

1973. During the same time women working full-time year-round made far too little progress: an average of $255 a year in 2007 dollars. They are still on average $10,000 per year behind men. Young workers, men and women together, earned ten percent less in 2007 than young workers earned in 1979.[2]

What is a full-time job anyway? It used to be 40 hours a week. That standard was not universal, but in 1976, half of working men 25 to 54 years old had a 40-hour week. By 1993, those who work a lot longer – 49 hours a week or more – went from 22 percent to 29 percent of all employees, while the percentage who worked 40 hours fell by the same amount.

Men starting their adult work life, age 16 to 25, have the opposite problem: they have a difficult time getting a full-time job. The percentage of them working less than 35 hours a week increased from 34 percent in 1976 to 40 percent in 1993.

Women age 25 to 54 just find themselves working too much. The proportion who are employed less than 40 hours a week fell, while those who put in 49 hours a week or more rose from 6 percent in 1973 to 12 percent in 1993.

Today, one out of six working persons puts in 49 hours or more a week, often more than 60 hours a week. Even the percentage of men and women 55 and over who work long hours increased. There is no rest for the weary. The stretchout happened in the same decades that

10

women entered the paid workforce, delivering a double whammy to family life.[3]

Dare we ask what went wrong?

Short-term ups and downs in the economy are one thing. Decades of working more and getting less are something else. The basic operation of the economy has switched onto a different track.

Despite the sputtering performance of the economic system, another feature of the past 35 years is the absence of any real push to reform it. In the accepted public realm – government, the press, the universities and think tanks, the trade unions, and political organizations of all kinds – there is no initiative to deal with the big downward drift.

Some people say we cannot do much of anything. They portray the economy like a solar system: the planets move in orbits around the sun, and you cannot change it.

Yes, there are laws of motion and development in society as well as in nature – but what is the economy if not the rules, agreements, and institutions that combine our work and distribute the fruit of our efforts? It is not easy for millions of people to change the setup, but no natural force prevents us from doing it.

Our leaders provide no vision of helpful change for the great majority who are working harder or unable to get a decent job, a majority who cope with more difficult lives than people experienced in 1973.

As long as there was economic progress for most, even though considerable numbers in every generation did not get their share, leaders in the public realm simply promised to keep it going, and that was good enough.

Common people suffered a horrible economic disaster in the 1930s. The public realm responded with a lot of serious improvising. The federal government's New Deal programs, regulations, and financial reforms stopped the decline, although they did not really get us growing again. World War Two (1941-1945) came along, and at the cost of blood and social sacrifice by millions, the economy geared up for war and found its way forward again.

Until the crash of 2008, the decline since 1973 has not been as sudden and dramatic as the Great Depression. Instead, a relentless grind has chewed up hope for decades. Life goes on, but where is the inspiring social vision? Where are the opportunities offered by economic progress, not for a handful of lucky entrepreneurs but for millions of people? What instills enthusiasm to create, build, and organize?

This essay is a search for answers. What went wrong, and what must we do about it?

One good thing about getting back to basics is that the answers turn out to be fairly simple. Endless complications are fascinating for experts who have time to master the details, but the economic system has a deep problem, and the solution is big but not complicated. In a phrase, it is the title of this essay: no rich, no poor.

The equality view of inequality

Statistics all over the place describe the huge gap between the rich and the rest of us. But neither the political establishment, policy intellectuals, nor professors tell us this:

If we took all the personal income in this country and paid it equally to everyone who wants a job, each of us would earn $72,000 a year for a full-time job. And by the way, there is enough left over to double all Social Security benefits, too. (The calculation is in the Appendix.)

The figure is for the year 2007. Naturally, $72,000 would grow with inflation. Does it ever need to shrink? That is, must there be such a thing as a big recession? Only if you accept that unemployment should rise and production fall not because of any natural disaster but because the economic and political system prevents human action.

Garrison Keillor, a story-teller with a dry sense of humor, spins tales about Lake Wobegon, the town where "all the children are above average." The town is imaginary, of course. We chuckle because usually the average is somewhere in the middle. The United States has become a society where most people have below-average incomes all or most of their lives.

13

It is not enough to look at the distribution of income for one year. The difference between the rich and the rest of us enlarges enormously over the working decades of a person's life. Someone who takes $300,000 a year for ten years gets as much as someone earning $72,000 is paid over 40 years.

On the other hand, some people exceed the equality line for a few peak years, but these are an exception time in their entire working life. Their income over a working lifetime does not average $72,000 a year.[4]

Because so few take so much, more than 90 percent of the population is kept below average income. These are the common people: most employees who have full-time jobs; the great majority of those who work part-time because that is all the work they can find; the unemployed; most small business operators; and most retired people.[5]

The rich often take enormous salaries, but that should not hide the importance of income obtained from "business." If workers in 2007 had somehow equalized pay among themselves, each of them would by definition have received the average, which the Census reports was $51,556 for full-time workers who worked 50 weeks or more – a lot less than $72,000.[6] The gap tells us that a huge amount of income flows to the rich through different channels. In addition to enjoying a "job" that pays an unreal amount per hour, the rich own stocks and collect dividends, do financial deals and make big money on Wall Street, hold bonds and collect interest, and govern large corporations with all the opportunities that control brings.[7]

Most people have not made the progress they could reasonably have expected in 1973. On the other hand, about one person in ten has done very well, and one person in ten thousand has raked in big riches. The money and power of a very few dominate the public realm, forbidding serious work on the growing list of economic problems that bear down on common people.

The rich have been around for a long time, although the income gap between them and the common people has rarely been so extreme as it is today. The rich have always lusted after more than they already have. They have always been willing to take more and more from most of us, although they usually tolerated a bit of reform when survival of the economic system, their golden goose, depended on it. We need to explain why the economy stopped working for common people about 35 years ago.

A century of hard-fought gains just stopped

Before 1973 the fruits of growth were certainly not divided equally, but shares in economic progress remained stable on the average. Since the economy grew in real ways – more food and clothing, broader education, more sanitary and comfortable housing, the freedom of motorized transportation, electric lighting and household appliances – life got better on the average. Some decades were good, some were depressions. There were bad times for the majority of working people, such as the 1920s, which were also a time of great prosperity for those who were already in the upper income ranks. After the 1920s and mid-1930s, life improved in the 1940s and 1950s for many people.

On average property income was 20% of the national product from 1870 to 1935. It fell during the latter 1930s and World War Two but then rose to old levels. From 1870 to 1930 the share of wages in national income rose from approximately 50% to 65%, but the increase was largely due to farmers and their children moving off the land and into the ranks of wage and salary workers in factories and offices.[8]

One person moved up the income ladder while another one slipped back, although there was much less mobility than we are usually led to imagine. Most of the gains captured by the majority of working people were the result of struggles like the big strikes in 1875-77, 1886 (for the eight-hour day), and 1892-94. The decade before World War One (1914-1918) was a time of Wobbly campaigns by down-and-out workers, and a million people voted for socialist presidential candidate Eugene Debs. In the 1930s workers won their biggest victory, industrial unions in the mass production industries: automobiles, rubber and tires, electrical appliances, steel and more.

By the 1930s most people had left the farm. Land ownership or a secure traditional right to land had been the foundation of family economic survival for centuries in this country and for thousands of years worldwide. Now most people held jobs but did not own land or other productive assets. Less than ten percent of the population had small businesses. There is no way that most people can have their own factories, offices, railroads and other transportation networks and so on.

A new foundation of economic security was needed. Bits and pieces of it were introduced: Social Security, unemployment and welfare benefits because the economy does not have enough jobs, and a right to health care (for everyone in most industrializing countries, but only for employees with stable jobs in the United States).

It was not accidental that the economy grew. Growth was a consequence of several forces, one of which was fights by common people for a better standard of living. Over the broad sweep of the hundred years or so up to 1973, common people succeeded in maintaining an approximately stable share of a growing economic pie. The owners of the big corporations at the heart of the industrializing economy kept pressing down on everyone else, then relenting a bit when faced with determined struggle.

Industrial capitalism prevailed in the United States from about 1870. Everyone knows businesses operate for the purpose of making money. They reinvest some of their profits to make more money. The investment cannot always be to make more of the same thing; the market for a particular product cannot expand indefinitely. Businessmen look for new products to sell. The result was that investment and growth went through a series of industries: cotton textiles, canned foods and refrigerated meat, farm machines, mass production of clothing, bicycles, breakfast cereals and snacks made from wheat and corn, automobiles, electrical lighting and all the wire and apparatus in the power grid, refrigerators and other household appliances, radios, and more.

When an industry stopped growing, just holding steady or fading away, another industry arose. It was all done with industrial labor. Workers operating machines in factories moved from the shrinking industry to the new one, or their children did. Gradually, too, white-collar staff in offices grew, although so did low-paying retail jobs. Nearly all the work was highly routinized. When things are done with machinery but the work is not fully automated, most of the labor of feeding and unloading machines is routine.

Big employers want to break work down as much as possible into routine labor. For one thing, unskilled and semiskilled workers are cheaper than highly trained craftsmen, mechanics, and engineers. For another, routine jobs are easier to fill from a large pool of potential employees. And as a matter of control, corporations want the know-how of their operations kept in the heads of just a few well-paid managers and specialists. Big businesses do not want to depend on most employees exercising judgment and skill derived from experience.

When businessmen smelled fat profits from new ventures, they were often willing to concede wage gains if workers mounted a strong fight. Workers got money to buy some of the things they produced. Although workers also won a shorter work week and some safeguards from dangerous machinery, most labor became more routinized.

The industrial revolution of the history books is the story of building an economy based on workers performing routinized labor around hugely productive machinery. Thread was no longer spun in the home; weavers no longer wove cloth in their own small shops. New industries provided farms with machinery that made millions of farmers' sons redundant; they left the land.

Industry helps science, then science helps industry

Another development was going on at the same time – deliberate, continual use of natural sciences for economic change. Back in the late 1700s, James Watt, an inventor of the steam engine, did not know the physics of heat and gases, because the theories largely did not exist. Instead, scientists played catchup, explaining how the steam engine worked after it became a major economic force. Scientists were often amateurs, not connected directly with business. By the beginning of the twentieth century, science and industry were coming closer, helping each other to advance in rapid steps. The corporate giants of the electrical, chemical, and photographic industries among others had their own research laboratories, devoted to using science as well as adding to it in order to create new products and whole new industries.

The invention and introduction of semiconductor transistors provides a good example of what was happening. Dr. J. Edgar Lilienfeld put together a transistor around 1923. He built a radio and showed it to corporations. They rebuffed his discovery. The electronics-based industries of the day, primarily radio and telephones, continued to use glass-housed vacuum tubes. Lilienfeld could not explain very clearly how or why his transistor worked, partly because quantum physics was just getting started. [9] The motion of electrons in vacuum tubes was better understood, which meant that scientists could more easily modify them, within limits, as needed for new products.

The transistor was re-invented at Bell Labs in 1947-48. By then the corporate parent, AT&T, in order to maintain the growth of long distance telephoning and offer it more affordably, badly wanted something better than vacuum tubes. Their power consumption, fragility, and fairly short life before failure (think of light bulbs) were obstacles. Bell Labs knew about much of the prior art in semiconductors; we do not know whether they were aware of Lilienfeld's work. Other scientists, inventors, and companies were in pursuit of similar goals, especially to make radar work better during World War Two. Bell Labs happened to be the winner, at least when it came to the Nobel Prize. One of the winning trio, physicist John Bardeen, was able to "develop a theory of the quantum surface states of electrons which led to the conclusion that a charge layer existed at the free surface of semiconductors."[10] William Shockley went on to do much the same for a variation, the junction transistor, which at the time was even easier to work with.

We all have some idea of the enormous impact of semiconductors, especially when they are put together as "chips," or integrated circuits on tiny slices of silicon or another semiconducting element. We are told less often about the economic change that appeared with semiconductor electronics. Unlike previous industrial growth, new electronics industries had significant economic impact without enlisting large armies of factory

21

operatives. Furthermore, the products of the these industries enabled machines to approach near-total automation in a whole series of old industries. Screw manufacturing, engine fabrication and many other metal-working processes needed far fewer workers. On all sorts of assembly lines, machines guided their own work and handed it off to the next machine. A photograph of an early Ford assembly line shows men crowded among the machines; a modern assembly line is mostly machinery, sparsely dotted along the way with human-staffed work stations.

Automation was widely discussed in the 1950s. By 1973 the understanding of natural science, and its ability to jump on a discovery and work out the "how-to" as a matter of theoretical understanding, or at least a standardized recipe, meant that never again would new industries need to hire large armies of semiskilled labor – at least, not at the going wage rate in industrial economy. (Later in this essay we will examine the global reach for new pools of extremely cheap labor.)

While routine labor was relentlessly being eliminated in factories and offices, new economic sectors did not offer lots of good jobs.

The nature of work has changed before. In the nineteenth century farm work shrank and industrial jobs multiplied by the millions. In the early twentieth century factory labor hit a plateau, and further job growth came in offices and stores. The changes were full of disaster for indi-

22

vidual workers, but overall the majority of working people won a stable share of the fruits of production.

Since 1973 the economic decline of routinized labor has left workers worse off. Most of the next generation, instead of being at the heart of the next great thing, find themselves flipping burgers and serving coffee as youth. Or they spend years in jobs well below their educational attainment before they get established in the work world. Too many older workers must postpone retirement and become greeters at Wal-Mart. In between youth and old age, the humdrum but stable career has disappeared. Life is lived with insecurity of employment and health care; comfortable housing is out of reach until much later in life if at all; and the goal of sending one's children to a good college is blocked by ever-higher financial hurdles. Inequality becomes greater, pushing more people down and narrowing the winners' circle to a few trophy finishers. More of them are children of the rich, along with a few lucky ones who happen to be in the right business at the right moment. The days of so-called hard work reliably rewarded with average prosperity are over.

Not that shove-it jobs are gone. Just the opposite, most work remains routinized. There is plenty of mindless to-and-fro in janitorial work, for example, but routinized labor has become separated from the front lines of the advance of human productiveness. The industrial revolution that started by reducing traditional farm and craft work to routinized labor leaves work in this subhuman form; only, now there is less reward.

When new industries needed masses of ready hands, working people could share in the gains. New industries still appear, but working people make continual concessions to get a job. What passes now for economic growth has two parts. One consists of islands of luck, often in high tech (rewarding a few of the many who go for the gold). The other part is about making a profit using cheap labor. The burger chains use high-tech cash registers tied into corporate-wide inventory networks, but the cashier does not read the menu; she punches a picture icon for the menu item that the customer wants.

We have described the economic arc of the last 150 years, but we have not explained the basic reason for the decline we are living through. To do that, we need to back up and take an even broader historical look.

The major turning points of history

The work people do in a capitalist economy has changed for two hundred years. People suffered great dislocation and deprivation, but the economy made the change, and there were rewards.

Today work is changing again, but with a difference. Growth based on industrial labor, yielding mass prosperity, began to break down several decades ago. Capitalism is unable to give way to the new institutions required to get beyond routinized jobs.

What comes next? We can find the answer by reviewing the big changes in work over the course of human history. Every time there was a big change in how and what people produce, new economic relations arose, too, at roughly the same time. We have arrived at one of the major turning points in work and the economic relations within which we all live. It will take us into the fifth major period of human life.

The first period lasted millions of years, but it can be regarded as preparation. Humans emerged as a distinct species and took up a new kind of life, separating themselves from the other animals forever. A mix of animal behavior and human labor changed in favor of the latter until it became almost 100 percent of what we are all about. This period ended about 40,000 years ago.

The second period, lasting 25,000 to 30,000 years in some parts of the earth and almost until today in other places, was a time of creating genuine economy. It was an economy of no rich, no poor.

Economic equality was gradually lost in the change to the third period. Starting around 10,000 years ago the overwhelming majority of people in a society worked the land and lived their life around the requirements of growing food and fiber. After several thousand years of this, their exploitation began.

Fourth, capitalism replaced peasant life with industrial labor starting about 500 years ago in Europe.

Now we must push through to the fifth period by recovering a social order of no rich and no poor, guaranteeing satisfaction of continually developing material needs, and providing everyone the basis to find happiness in work and therefore in life.

The long walk from animal behavior to human freedom

If I stand up, walk a few steps, pick up the telephone, and punch out a number, I owe gratitude to our ancestors who made it possible. They were animals, living as all animals do by instinctive and conditioned behavior. Deer graze, bees suck nutrients from flowers, lions hunt, and tree mammals grab nuts and fruit today as they have done for vast stretches of time, typically millions of years.

Within limits animals modify their behavior as changes of climate and surroundings compel them. They move geographically, and they apply the same grazing, sucking, or hunting routine to slightly different sources of food. Big changes in their lives under environmental pressure lead to evolution of a new species. Their bodies are different and so is their diet and the way they get what they eat. They survive but they do not become vastly more productive.

Chimpanzees and their primate ancestor foraged in trees, eating fruits, leaves and nuts. The change of species that interests us probably began when forests shrank during a climate change. Some primates came out of their group of trees, moving to the next clump where there might be more food. They could use their "hands" to hold nuts and fruit, perhaps wrap them in leaves, and make primitive tools out of small branches. The advantages of using hands were greater if one walked on two feet instead of knuckle-walking on feet and curled fingers. Erect walking further freed their hands to become marvelously capable, able to strike suitable stones against each other, making tools. With these implements they could cut and tear meat, get to the marrow in bones, and clean animal hides and wear them.[11]

Our ancestors worked sticks into pointed projectiles, then learned to lash amber or a shaped stone to the end, inventing the spear. Working as a group they could track, herd and, with a well-aimed and powerful thrust, kill the animal that was the source of meat. The eye had to look at the target, and the brain coordinated movement of the arm, as well as paying attention to the group's work and performing one's own moves in the hunting script. The brain evolved in size and power along with the tool-making and tool-using work of the hands.

Emerging humans had to feed children for years while preparing them for work with instruction by example and practice. This was not the job of one mother, nor of a mother aided by a father. They lived in a group of one or two dozen. At any one time the needs of the dependent children were met by all the adults together, sharing food and child-rearing duties.

This evolution began around five million years ago. Stone tools are known from two and half million years ago. Some time after, humans in the making revolutionized their attitude to fire.

Overcoming justified fear of its ravages, they discovered and felt the triumph of using contained fire that did not start a conflagration. Meat could be cooked, and some of it kept.

The sounds these humans uttered to coordinate their activity made refined vocal cords an advantage for survival. Useful exchange of sounds trained the ear and brain to distinguish them carefully. About 100,000 years ago these humans made the leap to language. Sounds did more than signal observation of an object of food or a dangerous animal. They became symbols populating a new mental world. With language things can be recalled from the past, imagined with variations on their reality, as well as grouped and compared.

Language has a grammar that breaks out of the confines of several hundred signals. Grammar, not learned as rules but unconsciously obeyed, makes possible infinite combination of core sounds into sentences. Languages have from a dozen to more than a hundred sounds, clustering around an average of three dozen. Sentences state what was, what is, and what might be, and conversely what was/is/will not be, as well as what should have been or not and should be or should not be.

By 40,000 years ago human beings were biologically equivalent to us. If we had a time machine and could go back to that era and return with a newborn baby, we could raise it like any child. He or she could walk on two feet to the telephone, pick it up, remember a number, and punch the buttons to dial it. That person could talk to someone with the same power of speech and language we have, too.[12]

Gathering, gardening, farming

While biological development shrank to minor increase of height, loss of body hair and such, cultural progress quickened. Humans lived in a way that no animal lives: by social labor. Then, as now, they got what they needed from nature not by finding and taking it, but by making tools. With tools they hunted and dug, and they prepared what they had acquired or killed. They divided different kinds of tool-making and tool-using among the members of their community, pooling and allocating the fruits of productive labor. At most they had stories about their community arrangements, not a social theory, but they performed specific acts of labor consciously. They formed a mental representation of what must be done before they did it – a plan. It could therefore be imagined as a somewhat different plan, talked about, and perhaps modified and tried. A pride of lions hunts together and is social, but most of the aspects of social labor just mentioned are absent.

In particular, only human labor changes when people, noticing what happens while they work and coming up with variations, make a new tool and try a new labor process. The change is difficult. It must overcome inertia, superstition, and comfort with what has succeeded before and usually works. Nonetheless, human labor has changed at an increasing pace from one period to the next. To be sure, 40,000 years ago humans could not make telephones. They lived as gatherers, scavengers, and hunters. The changes from their day to ours are changes in social labor, in the how-to of making and using tools and in the raw materials worked on, and also in the organization of work with all its consequences for the whole set of social relationships and activities.

Within this second period of human history there was a great change in social labor, carried out in two steps. Around 13,000 years ago gathering, scavenging, and hunting were no longer enough to sustain a growing population. People had become too good at hunting! They had filled up all the territories available to them (at the density that gathering and hunting supports), and they reduced the population of their prey too much. The end of an ice age, by warming the climate and submerging food territories under rising seas, may have compelled changes, too. Needing food for more mouths, people devoted additional labor to harvesting, storing, and cooking wild cereals, and then to a technique they had been familiar with for a long time – gardening (horticulture), the ancestor of farming.[13]

Put seeds or roots in the ground, take care of them for a few weeks or months, and you can harvest wheat or other starches as well as protein vegetables like peas. People were led to domesticate useful wild plants they already knew about, selecting seeds for the next crop.

Furthermore, growers learned that turning the ground with a hoe of stone or bone increased the number and vigor of the plants tremendously. The domestication of flax provided a fiber crop. It could be woven to make cloth, much as grasses had already been woven, sometimes replacing hides and furs. Soon after the taming of wheat, animals were domesticated for milk in addition to the meat, hides, and bones already used by hunters.

Although those who live by gathering and hunting make tools and are already human, separated from all other animals by a wide gap, hoe farmers have more of what we call an economy. They must reserve part of the crop for seeds to plant again. They store most of the harvest, consuming it over several months until the next crop is ready. They found improvements by repeated observation and pondering in the course of practical activity. Farming and other work became more productive, and the community could store food for several years as a reserve in case of a crop failure. The society had wealth.

Villagers did not need all their labor time to grow crops and take care of goats, sheep, pigs, or cattle. The people of this era discovered how to make pottery. They worked wood into implements, furniture, and structures far more intricate than could be made with stone, although not as long-lasting. They remembered these activities, distilling practical craft knowledge of materials and what you can do with them.

Just as in the gathering and hunting era, life was cooperative and people were equal. Clearing land, harvesting crops, and building residence halls required the combined effort of villagers. As for equality, village graves from this era are all of the same material level; as it was in life so it was in death. During the first, preparatory period of millions of years, and in most of the second period of several tens of thousands of years, small bands of people had no choice: everyone worked and received about the same share of food, clothing, and shelter.

People were perfectly capable of achieving happiness even though greed, avarice, and ruthless climbing to the top of the heap were economically impossible. As we shall see in a moment, a reliable surplus could enable some persons to contribute no productive labor yet consume far more than everyone else – but it did not happen right away. If selfishness were inherent in an unchanging human nature, humans would never have developed or they would have died off long ago.

The final step in this second period saw the most rapid increase in productive powers and wealth yet seen. During two or three thousand years garden farming became real agriculture. This was done by irrigation in a few large river valleys or by using a plow. Deep tillage of the earth dramatically increases the crop. In many societies of the time the plow had a metal tip. An independent industry, mining and smelting metal ores, and the allied industry of casting and molding metal, gave a big boost to the farming sector. Early metals were copper and its alloy with tin, bronze. However, widespread use of metal in farming arrived with the making of iron a thousand or so years later.

The division of labor changed, too. The division in gardening villages was one of activity among people who nearly all did the same rounds of raising crops and hunting for meat, at least among the men as a group and among the women as a group. After awhile the village smith might be a full-time specialist.

With full agriculture as opposed to horticulture, however, society grows beyond the village, although it remains the site of most people's lives. An important small percentage of the society could be detached from farming and engage in specialized crafts, such as pottery on the fast potter's wheel (another major invention of the time), woodworking, stone masonry, and metal smelting and smithing.

The agrarian order

When social organization expanded beyond the limit of a village, it became more complex. Certain lucky groups had the opportunity to become exploiters. Sooner or later they took it. In the sprawling river basins of Egypt and Sumeria (now Iraq), those who kept a planting calendar and organized work on irrigation canals in the slack season turned themselves into priests, laying a burden of religion on the peasants. Sincerity of belief is not the issue here. Religion refers to an organized social enterprise with a set of ideas about life as a whole that are propagated for social control. This institution is different from personal thoughts and conclusions about the world people found themselves in. For a long time before religion was organized, people wondered about the big questions of life and death. They had social norms of right and wrong. They had stories of how the world came into being and notions of what it "really" is.

In other places military leaders converted themselves into kings. With retainers and officials they formed an exploiting class of one variety or another.

They were all exploiters. That is, they did little or no labor to produce material wealth, which is what peasants and craftsmen do, yet each one of them consumed more stuff than a working person. It was more stuff in the sense that their fine food, clothes, and housing, not to mention all sorts of luxuries, took more hours and day of labor to make than was spent in producing the food, clothing and such of the working people.

The great majority of the people worked on the land, growing crops, raising animals, and engaging in a variety of domestic crafts.

This is the third period, the era of agrarian exploitation.

From Egypt when pyramids were built 5,000 years ago to China right until 1949, most people performed basically the same kind of work and suffered under variations of the same kind of exploitation. This is true despite the variety of civilizations that appeared and disappeared in those millennia: the Roman empire; the Church and kings of medieval Europe; the Sumerian, Persian, Arab, and Ottoman empires around the Middle East and Asia Minor; the civilizations of India; the series of dynasties in China; and the Mayan, Inca, Aztec, and other kingdoms in what is now Latin America. Just as we see more variety in the flowers of plants than in their stalks and roots, the rich during the era of agrarian exploitation spent their wealth in a variety of ways, but most people did much the same kind of labor and were exploited in re-markably similar ways.

Seventy to ninety percent of the population lived on the land. Farming was their main work, which must follow the rhythms laid down by nature. Besides tilling and harvesting for food and fiber, people met most of their needs by their own hand applied to domestic crafts and industries. They worked in small groups, which at one or another locale were nuclear families, wider kinship groups, or village groups. Although the term has more specific meanings, we refer to the working people as the peasants.[14]

The exploiters took a huge bite of the peasants' crops for pyramids, wars, whatever. The obligation might have started in ancient times with customary gifts to tribal chiefs for their protection. It might be called taxes paid to the government. It might be paid to a landlord. In all cases the exploiters made sure they got their take, but for the most part they left the details of farming to the village or the individual peasant. It is not easy to ride herd on the labor of peasants. The lord often had the authority, but the economic cost of supervision was too high.[15]

In the period of agrarian exploitation the exploiters were not involved in close oversight of production. They did not worry daily about which line of industry to put their money in, because the great majority of wealth was tied to land-based exploitation, supplemented by a few non-agricultural industries (mining, metalworking, perhaps pottery and brick works), all of it operated in traditional ways that were slow to change.

As long as the peasants handed over rent or taxes, the exploiters did not get involved. In the Roman world, for example, a master kept a dozen or two hands on a farm and hired an overseer to run it. A rich man like Cicero owned several small farms in his native region plus estates in seven or eight other places; a very wealthy owner would have dozens of farms, each about 75 to 100 acres.[16] In some situations the exploiters dictated what crops peasants were to grow, especially if they were officially slaves. (Commercial slavery on the large cotton plantations of the U.S. South in the nineteenth century, as well as the earlier Caribbean and Brazil sugar plantations, is a completely different animal.) However, slavery was never characteristic of an entire society. With rare regional exceptions slaves were a small minority of the working people.

One class worked; the other class disdained labor and the dirty details of growing a crop, making things, and mining. The exploiters were the rulers, and they engaged in political struggle and wars. They lived lives of leisure and luxury. The rulers watched that things did not get out of hand. State-sanctioned or state-allied religious institutions have taught many things in different societies, all of it bullying the minds of the peasants with superstition and the inevitability of their position on earth.

The gap between peasants and exploiters sometimes became enormous. At the end of the Roman Republic in the first century BC, "the income differential between rich and poor approximated a minimum of 1,200 to 1 and a maximum of 20,000 to 1, in contrast to a probable ratio of several hundred to 1 of ancient Athens after the Peloponnesian War."[17]

Similarly, a mere 23,000 scholar-officials were the lords of the Ming and Qing dynasties of China (1368 to 1911). The population grew from 90 million to 400 million people, but they were kept living near subsistence. The officials, owning a quarter of all land, took 19 percent of agricultural output as rent plus the rewards of office: fees, bribes, mandatory gifts, and on and on. But that was only half the peasants' burden. Local landlords, sitting in tea houses in the towns, received another hefty chunk of the peasants' rice and other output as rent.[18]

Civilization without a better life

The speed of social change has increased from one major stage to the next. Agrarian exploitation lasted about 5,000 years. That is a short time compared to the previous stages of human society, but still longer than one might have expected. About 2,000 years ago productive techniques for a new order had developed. Plows built partly with iron, so that they went deep and turned over the soil, were used in both Europe and China, although not universally. The waterwheel and windmill, two sources of power that did not have to be fed like people and animals, were known but not widely applied. Yet agrarian ways went on for another fifteen to twenty centuries.

No dynamic within the agrarian economy drove it to revolutionize the labor performed by most people. In many societies there was not even a gradual trend to a better standard of living on the basis of greater productive powers. Productiveness often stagnated. When it advanced – for example, more productive rice strains were bred in China – the additional crop usually fed more people. They had to live at pretty much the same subsistence level.

The exploiting class held back and suppressed basic advances in the productiveness of labor. They consumed potential investment wealth in non-productive pursuits. The peasants grew food to support the exploiters, their retainers, state officials, and priests or monks. As for urban craftsmen, most of their labor was channeled to making luxury goods and weapons for the rich rather than supplying peasants with a growing stream of improved plows and other useful tools.

The rich were absorbed in socially unproductive activities. At various times and places a powerful king or emperor compelled nobles to compete for place by ostentatious shows at court. At other times the armies of local warlords fought each other endlessly. In Egypt enormous crews of oppressed people were conscripted to build pyramids – supersized monuments to dead lords and pharaohs that contributed nothing to peasants' lives. During much of Chinese history the rich maintained a highly refined literary society that sucked up the talent and energy of bright young men. There was more social waste in the mutual gift-giving, bribery, and entertainment required to maintain and advance a family's place among the rich.

A good portion of social wealth went to keeping the peasants in their place. There were local police forces as well as central armies ready to move around the empire wherever rebellion had to be crushed. Resources were poured into religious ceremonies and public feasts in the ancient Middle East and Greece, magic shows in the Roman world to befuddle with superstition, and the massive machinery of the Church in the European middle ages.[19]

How the agrarian order lasted thousands of years

It was obvious how exploiters got their riches. They did not want fewer peasants toiling over crops. They might want the same number of peasants to use better seeds, producing more wheat and cotton. They might want a bigger population of peasants to grow more. But the exploiters wanted to keep peasants working on the land. That was the source of the exploiters' wealth. At times oligarchies took so much from the peasants that they killed the goose laying their eggs. Whole regions might be depopulated – but agrarian lords never pioneered a new economic system.

There were, however, different ways to maintain agrarian exploitation. A strong contrast exists between Europe before 1300 and China throughout its millennia of imperial dynasties.

In England a peasant household might prosper more than others for awhile, but in general the equality of earlier times carried over to agrarian society. The concrete evidence is the near-universal system of dividing the arable land of a village into strips and assigning them to maintain equality among households. Each one farmed the strips assigned to it and took the harvest. Households were kept in rough equality to each other by periodic re-allocation of strips, matching the mouths and hands of a family to a number of strips as well as rotating the more fertile sections of the village land. Strip assignments were re-done every year (in other parts of Europe every twelve or twenty years) and when a household died out.[20] A communal feature fitted to the strip system was plowing by a team of oxen, typically eight of them. The team, perhaps assembled from several households, plowed all the village strips one after another.

From 500 to 1000 A.D. English lords developed the power of serfdom over the peasants, using it to keep them in their villages and extracting tribute and labor service. Serfdom rode high until 1300 A.D. It was an institution for perpetuating agrarian exploitation.

In China a bureaucratic empire kept agrarian exploitation going centuries after it disintegrated in England and western Europe. Villages as a collective had little say over the use of land. It was a matter of direct relation between peasant families and landlords, subject to edicts and allocations of state-owned land by the imperial bureaucracy. Most peasants lived at subsistence. If a peasant household managed to prosper, two opportunities lured. The head of the family might buy land and become a landlord, or he supported a son who spent years preparing for the scholars' examinations in Chinese classical literature and culture. If the son scored a passing grade at the local, provincial, or national cutoff, he made the hiring list for a position in the corresponding level of government. What a banquet the family would have then!

China from the Song dynasty (it began in 960 A.D.) gives us an example of the ruling class applying deliberate policy to suppress threatening tendencies toward industrial development. It began with an agricultural change. Before 750 A.D. two-thirds of the people lived in the dry wheat-farming areas of northern China. By 1150 A.D. two-thirds of the people, now doubled in number, lived in irrigated rice-farming areas of south China. New strains of rice, a technique of growing three crops a year, and other agricultural improvements were encouraged through an imperial network of agricultural extension offices.[21] Some people left the land. During the eleventh century as much a fifth of the population lived in cities and towns.[22] Farmers sold output at markets. Merchants became more prominent, although the imperial bureaucracy always kept the upper hand over them. Despite the advance in farm productiveness, peasants were kept near a survival standard of living. There were simply more of them.[23]

Shoots of capitalism were sprouting as fast as bamboo, but imperial officials ripped them out. They put industrial workshops producing salt, weapons, porcelain wares, bricks and more under state control. Officials and landlords who explored business operations were steered back, without much resistance, into buying land and competing to keep official positions in their family. Increased rent and taxes on the peasants returned prosperous families to subsistence level. Finally, a rule that all sons inherited the family land by dividing it kept holdings small.

Although Chinese craftsmen are credited with inventing gunpowder, paper, printing, the navigational compass, and other technological advances, handicraft labor was not applied in a mass way to manufacture new and useful things for the peasants. Just the opposite, inventions were used to serve the rich, amuse them, and strengthen their rule.

Agrarian kingdoms and empires arose and fell one after another. At the core of these stories is the degree of agrarian exploitation. Peasant revolts against unbearable conditions often toppled dynasties in China. A soldier leader would become the new emperor. He would temporarily reduce the tax and rent burden, pay more attention to river dikes and canals, and administer grain storage and disbursement when famine struck. Then mandarin bureaucrats would give in to luxury and sloth, letting infrastructure decay and squeezing more from the peasants. It was a historical cycle.

In the Mediterranean region, the Roman empire collapsed under assault by barbarians largely because exploitation of the peasants became so extreme. The rich wasted and destroyed the very source of their power. The underlying economy remained much the same. Over centuries new political powers replaced the Romans. Persian, Arabic, and Turkish rulers, like the Romans before them, existed by agrarian exploitation.

On the working side of the great divide within these societies, nothing compelled peasants to move beyond agrarian economy. Security of food, shelter, and clothing was their first concern. The best assurance was to have land to farm, freedom to grow food and fiber for themselves, and tolerable rent and taxes.[24] These levies were almost always paid by handing over a chunk of the harvest and by performing forced labor or military service. When these exactions were high, the peasants had little beyond subsistence, few means to make a better life.

Peasants always knew that their life of farming along with domestic and village industry would be prosperous if not for the taxes, rents, tithes and other levies, if not for the arbitrary violence of the nobles, if not for wars between factions of the rich sweeping through their land. During the early centuries of agrarian exploitation there must have been a memory in the villages of the previous era of agricultural labor when all were roughly equal in work and in enjoyment of its fruits.

In fact, at times peasants enjoyed bearable obligations. For example, the collapse of the Roman empire left nobles in parts of Europe less able to extort from the peasants.[25] They enjoyed better lives, ate more, and perhaps worked a bit less (farming by hand or behind a horse or an ox is exhausting toil). They enjoyed their prosperity more or less together. It was a happier life, not a way of life headed for upheaval and disappearance in an industrial revolution.

Conditions for the end of agrarian exploitation

The regime of agrarian exploitation did not compel exploiters or peasants to go beyond the existing mode of work. Exploiters actively opposed threatening economic advances, while their use of wealth was anything but economically progressive. On the other side, the peasants wanted a pure agrarian life.

The unstoppable end to the historical era of agrarian exploitation occurs when three conditions prevail.

One, the level of productiveness must develop to the point that a good number of working people are not needed in farming.

Two, some peasants must be able to keep more of their crops and other products than the subsistence minimum.

Three, social limits on inequality among the peasants must break down so that on one hand rich peasants appear and acquire more land than their family can work, and on the other hand some peasants become so short of land and even landless that they must hire themselves out at least part of the time.

Eventually, much of the agrarian world met the first condition. The productive power that England and parts of Europe, China, and other societies attained by 1300 was significantly greater than it was when agrarian society began thousands of years earlier. In Europe "the Middle Ages changed the face of industry. ... water, wind and animal power were doing many things for which previously only human muscles were available."[26] In China, as we saw, population and the production of rice and wheat to feed them doubled and doubled again. There was real advance, though much slower than we are used to in a capitalist economy.

The real hurdles are the second and third conditions.

In China the second condition – peasant power to reduce exploitation that kept them at subsistence – never went far enough. The rule of officials and landed gentry over a vast land and 100 million people by the year 1300 was strong enough to keep the peasants as a whole just above hunger. Even though farm productiveness rose with new rice strains and intensive use of human labor, the exploiting classes took the gains and spent them without undermining their system of extracting wealth from peasants.

After the Roman empire, European rulers never had the same power to exploit. There was no single empire across western and central Europe like the Chinese dynasties. In some parts of Europe serfdom was as oppressive in its own way as Chinese bureaucratic imperial rule, but not overall. Nor is it surprising that the economic order that would succeed European agrarian exploitation appeared around 1300 in an outlying island country of five million people.

In England the conditions for a new economic order finally became realities. Land and labor polarized into new classes: rich peasants, some of them on their way to becoming capitalist, and poor peasants on their way to becoming wage workers. There were enough of both, although most peasants remained in the middle. The rich peasants had surplus wealth and sought ways to use it for additional advantage. The poor peasants did not have enough land to farm, or enough animal power to plow it (this task used to be communal).

It took three centuries of turmoil, wars, upheavals in government, and mass uprisings, but by 1600 England was on an unstoppable road to a capitalist economy. There were still more small producers who were self sufficient in farming, a craft business, or a small shop than there were capitalists, but there was no going back to the binding ties of agrarian exploitation.

For all we can tell, agrarian exploitation might have continued for hundreds of years, perhaps another thousand years. True, an economy is always changing. People consider how labor might be more productive. And there is always something to consider, because the experience of labor, of human arrangements imposed on natural processes, reveals new possibilities, curiosities that disclose new ways of producing. Such development has plenty arrayed against it – mental laziness, tradition, and economic interests that would suffer from change – but so long as people must produce in order to meet their needs, the push to economic development is unavoidable. However, the pace may be measured in decades, centuries, or millennia.

Still, no internal dynamic pushed the regime of agrarian exploitation along the line of development. No single river of cause and effect brought forth the next order. The waters of change sloshed around, eventually eroding a channel that descended into a new economic landscape.

Capitalism would prove to be just the opposite. It is governed by a core of basic economic laws.

Capitalist history moves along an unavoidable course to the regime that must succeed it.

Capitalism

Capitalism introduced a new way of exploiting those who do the work, one destined to turn their labor and lives upside down.

The end of feudalism in England was marked by events that ousted poor and middle level peasants – eventually, nearly all of them – from their land. One method was the enclosure of farm land and its conversion into sheep pasture, enforced by Parliament.

The land thieves were often the sons of feudal lords. They did not have the political power over villages that they used to, but they stole and tricked their way into private ownership of land. Then they rented it out to rich peasants and commercial farmers, who hired workers –.often peasants who had lost their land. The employer-farmers were now the active economic users of the soil, and they sold the crop on the market for money. For them the important thing was to grow as much crop as possible at the lowest cost, hence with the fewest possible workers.

These economic actors broke up agrarian exploitation and replaced it with agriculture as a business: running an enterprise with employees, selling the output, and aiming to maximize the excess of revenue over cost. Most peasants had no assets for entering a new line of industry.

They scraped by with occasional jobs, begging, or highway robbery. Some became full-time hired workers. Their children most definitely became workers.

In a capitalist society the core of the exploited is all those who need a job in order to live – workers. They do not have the assets required to make things and find customers to buy them, so they need a job. Somebody else (later, an institution like a corporation) owns the land, factory, store, or office with all the necessary equipment and funds. The employer hires workers to produce things or perform services. The worker gets a wage or salary. When the customer pays for the product or service, the money goes to the seller – the employer.

The employer-employee relationship is opposite to agrarian exploitation. The capitalist takes control of production, not waiting for the peasant to hand over rent after harvest. It is the capitalists' farm and equipment, his factory, his operation. Therefore, the crop, the cloth from the loom, the product belongs to him, but he also bears all the costs of production. His vital interest is the rate of profit: net gain per dollar invested.

Princes, warlords, absentee landlords, and mandarin bureaucrats of agrarian exploitation avoided economic management. Politics and war were their focus. True, they enforced their No to unwelcome development, and they saw to some general economic functions through their state, like managing rivers for crop irrigation and spreading new seeds. The peasants in their villages did not go to work every day for the lord. They grew crops pretty much on their own, handing over a chunk of it to pay rent and taxes. Sometimes peasants had to supply labor to work the lord's land and build roads and such. These obligations were distinct from both slavery and wage labor.

At first in family firms the capitalist runs all aspects of the business. Even later when managers supervise every aspect, big owners must pay attention to economic competition. In 2003 the Galvin family that founded Motorola 75 years earlier turned over the chief executive spot to an outsider after three generations. In 2006 the Ford family named a chief executive from outside their family. They had to in an attempt to preserve their ticket to riches.

The rulers of capitalism also engage in politics and wage wars, but their greater involvement in economic problems than agrarian exploiters is apparent here, too. The government has a big role outlawing trade unions or confining what they can legally do; deciding what health care people get; and resolving the struggle between old and new industries (for example, automobiles versus railroads and mass transit, and hard-wired versus wireless phones). International affairs under capitalism go well beyond the agrarian goals of commanding tribute and establishing trade in spices and wine. The goals are opening new markets; pumping oil and building pipelines; and, in the era of globalization, transferring factory work to low-wage regions.

Work under capitalism is not confined to the small scope and traditional methods practiced within the confines of a village under agrarian exploitation. The number of workers who labored under the will of a single capitalist operation expanded from small workshops in the 1600s and 1700s to factories with tens, hundreds, and thousands of workers. In the middle 1800s family firms gave way to corporations that orchestrate activity in dozens of factories, warehouses, and offices.

Craft methods taken over from the peasant era were broken down into pieces and recombined in shops with a division of labor, each worker doing one or two steps in a series. Then machines performed some of these steps. By the mid-twentieth century, the whole way of making things began to be done by an integrated complex of machines rather than by a team of workers and machines.

In these ways capitalism developed production so that we have a variety and abundance of clothes, not the single hemp or linen garment that a peasant typically wore for days on end. The peasant rarely left his village; now we cover miles daily by motor power on the land and occasionally in the air and across the seas. Almost no family makes what it consumes, but the working class as a whole makes all these things.

Individual workers spend their wages to buy what they need or want or are convinced they want. The total wages of all workers buy from corporations and other businesses a portion of what the working class made.

How the hard-fought gains stopped

Capitalism routinized daily labor. Hands-on work used to combine doing and understanding. No more. The worker became like a machine, repeating rote operations endlessly. Where the peasants managed their work by family and by village of which they were a part, employees are given detailed instructions and clocked to the second, or they are handed part of a total project, hemmed in with tight constraints, then called on to figure it out and do it by deadline.

Large capitalist operations have no choice. They must break down most of the work into little fragments of routinized labor and divide it up into unskilled or semiskilled jobs, jobs that rely as little as possible on the intelligence, devotion, experience, and developed skills of the human beings slotted into these positions.

Companies must minimize the cost of their products and services. Skilled labor costs more than semiskilled or unskilled labor. More important, skilled workers have more control over the pace of their work, how they do it, the quality of the product and even its specific nature. The boss can give them orders, but they are not as easy to replace as less skilled workers. This is another major reason why most jobs under capitalism cannot be skilled work. A capitalist economy functions by hiring from large pools of workers who can soon perform jobs that are designed not to require specific varieties of high skill.

Here is how federal government analysts define skilled, semiskilled and unskilled work:

—*Skilled* means workers of relatively high skill level having a thorough and comprehensive knowledge of the processes involved in their work. These workers exercise considerable independent judgment and usually receive an extensive period of training.

—*Semiskilled* means workers who operate machine or processing equipment or perform other duties of intermediate skill level which can be mastered in a few weeks and require only limited training.

—*Unskilled* means workers in occupations which generally require no special training to perform elementary duties that may be learned in a few days and require the application of little or no independent judgment.[27]

The emphasis is on judgment, a worker's assessment of the specific task and the pros and cons of handling it one way or another. Skilled work requires a knowledgeable eye that notices crucial details, making appropriate adjustments that determine the success and quality of the result. Judgment and skillful work are founded on comprehensive knowledge – scientific knowledge where it exists – and reflection on experience. Such reflection must be thoughtful. It must also be purposive, eager to produce the best result as regularly as possible and, from time to time, creating an advance in the quality and potency of the product and in the productiveness of the labor that creates it.

Actually, the hidden emphasis of the federal definitions is the opposite, an emphasis on *avoiding* these human attributes. As much as possible the capitalist employer removes judgment from most jobs. He prefers that only a few workers, separated as engineers or other professionals, provide the expertise. It is even better if the whole process can be put into machines.

The definitions are meant for factory and manual labor, but the same concepts apply to office and store work. True, sociologists are often reluctant to extend the terms this way. They believe and cultivate the notion that office work is superior to working with things. No matter how the occupational ladder is labeled, the ladder concept pervades occupational classification. The federal department of labor, looking back at its statistical work, summed up, "Occupations ... were arranged in a hierarchical system that corresponded, more or less, with skill and training level and socioeconomic status."[28]

Why? "An occupation is a group of jobs in which workers perform similar tasks, duties, or activities at similar skill levels."[29] Right away the report adds, "the occupational structure in the workplace ... provides a framework for descriptive occupational statistics, such as employment levels, job openings, earnings, and education."[30] In other words, skill levels have a lot to do with labor costs. By dividing the production task into jobs that sit lower on the occupational ladder, the employer has a wider pool of jobseekers and can bargain harder to pay them less.

The definitions above are from a government that serves employers. Semiskilled workers know there is more to their work. They learn to avoid little moves that would foul up the whole job. They find shortcuts and figure out better ways to do things. Employers recognize this reality when they prefer to hire someone who has experience in the industry, paying slightly higher wages. The fact remains that most jobs draw from a broad pool of potential employees. The great majority of the national workforce falls into several large categories: factory workers, retail staff, office workers, health care attendants, and a few more.

There is a lie in the term "semiskilled." It dangles the hope that the job is a stepping stone to skilled work. Back in 1948, Webster's Dictionary, Second Edition, defined semiskilled as "having some trade skill, but less than that of one who has served apprenticeship." Most factory and assembly line workers, as well as office employees, never got that opportunity to serve an apprenticeship. The term was promoted while craft occupations, which were indeed filled by training apprentices, were shrinking in the workforce. Meanwhile, the advanced education that someone needed to become an engineer, for instance, was out of reach of most employees, too. Dead-end factory jobs and office drudgery were expanding occupations. An expert in the U.S. Census, Alba Edwards, put these jobs into a statistical slot, giving it the hopeful name of semiskilled at the same time.[31]

We call it *industrial labor*. An industrial system of production makes work into a routine activity, drained of craft, as confined as a cog in a machine.

Production is usually repetition of a process in order to make lots of the output. The items are all basically the same thing, although each one may have a different color, size, and other characteristics within a fixed range of variety. Once the process is defined, the capitalist employer wants a combination of machines and employees to make lots of a well-defined assortment of things. The machines go through the same cycle over and over, and semiskilled workers are supposed to repeat a set of fairly simple chores, too. Bureaucratic office routines are similarly repetitive. Where there is repetition, work can be reduced to industrial labor.

Industrial labor was imposed before the industrial revolution

For hundreds of years capitalism has made labor more industrial. It happened long before mechanization. The word "manufacture" comes by way of old French from the Latin *manu factus*, literally, made by hand. With rare exceptions, manufacture during the 1600s and 1700s in England and some European countries did not use machines. They came later. The capitalist manufacturing operation, however, broke down both peasant side occupations and skilled artisan crafts into a series of routinized detail operations. It might take someone awhile to learn the knack of executing a certain twist of a tool, but then he did that and nothing else all day long. Instead of one watchmaker making all the parts and putting them together, adjusting the fit along the way, each employee in a watchmaking manufactory stamped out one or a few parts or put two or three of them together. Watches, previously curiosities for the nobility, became affordable for businessmen and their wives.

Writing in the late 1700s, Adam Smith said that a man who made ordinary pins, from drawing wire to forming and attaching a head to it, might make 20 a day. Smith is famous for describing the division of labor in making pins, claiming that a crew of ten men in a row, each repeating one or two operations, could make 48,000 pins a day, or 4,800 per man.[32]

Smith grants that pin making is "a very trifling manufacture," but he surveyed his world, "In every improved society, the farmer is generally nothing but a farmer; the manufacturer, nothing but a manufacturer. The labor too which is necessary to produce any one complete manufacture, is almost always divided among a great number of hands. How many different trades are employed in each branch of the linen and woollen manufactures, from the growers of the flax and the wool, to the bleachers and smoothers of the linen, or to the dyers and dressers of the cloth!"[33]

In Smith's world the farmer and manufacturer were employers, not workers. Spinning, weaving, and sewing had been domestic occupations of peasant wives, part of a day filled with a hundred tasks. The peasants' work was long and tiring, but it was not deadly monotonous. Manufacture made money for capitalist owners, while the people doing the work often looked back to the previous economic order, with good reason. They found themselves earning much less than feudal guild craftsmen, and they lived meaner lives than peasants. For the employer, the importance of a division of hand labor was not primarily a gain in employees' dexterity at a narrow task. The profit was in enforcing a relentless pace of work on every employee under a threat of being replaced by someone equally unskilled, something difficult to do when a single craftsman makes the whole product.

After workers were reduced to repetition, employers during the industrial revolution of the late 1700s to the twentieth century engaged in replacing them with machines. The essential difference of a machine from a tool is not the steam or electrical power that drives it. The user of a tool wields it with skill, for example coordinating hand and eye and knowing just when and where to execute a deft maneuver. Sometimes manual skill is not primary, but judgment is key. The beer brewer (typically a farm woman in the colonial United States) knew by sight, smell, and taste how long to boil the wort and how much to let it cool down. A machine takes skill and judgment into itself. To invent a machine meant figuring out, sometimes with science but mostly with lots of trial and error, how a device can replace a skilled person. The quality of the product often suffers. The machine process cannot duplicate skilled work, and the capitalist puts cost reduction above quality. Think of puffed white bread from an industrial oven as long as a city block.

In nearly all cases jobs of operating machinery are kept unskilled or semiskilled, partly by the degree of achievable mechanization but especially by design of the capitalist and the few engineers he hires. Semiskilled workers tend machines, feed them, turn on the start switch, and read meters or listen for bells telling when to stop a process and remove a batch.

The essence of the change from the division of labor in hand-based manufacturing to machine-based production – as far as the capitalist is concerned – was stated by Andrew Ure in his 1835 book with the title, pompous in his hands, *The Philosophy of Manufactures*. He summed up Adam Smith's observation that because some manufacturing jobs were more difficult while others were easier, so "to each [job] a workman of appropriate value and cost was naturally assigned."[34]

Ure complained on behalf of employers, "By the infirmity of human nature it happens that the more skillful the workman, the more self-willed and intractable he is apt to become." Therefore, "wherever a process requires peculiar dexterity and steadiness of hand, it is withdrawn as soon as possible from the cunning workman" and done by a machine "so self-regulating that a child may superintend it." The goal is to "reduce the task of work-people to the exercise of vigilance and dexterity." [35] The unchanging goal whether in hand-based manufacturing work-shops or mechanized factories is to use the lowest capabilities of human beings. That is the capitalist way to keep labor costs down.

Fifty years later Frederick Taylor, another theoretician scheming how to get the most out of workers, developed methods of managing work-ers based on using as little as possible of human capability. Taylor is known as the leader of the stop-watch gang, the observers with watch and clipboard who conduct so-called time and motion studies of people at work. Then they figure out detailed instructions directing how to do every instant of the job, extracting the maximum energy per hour from the employee.

Although many of Taylor's specific methods are particular to kinds of factory work that have almost disappeared today, his general principles remain relevant to the capitalist goal of routinizing labor.

Taylor asserted, "The science which underlies each act of each workman is so great and amounts to so much that the workman who is best suited to actually doing the work is incapable of fully understanding this science, without the guidance and help of those who are working with him or over him, either through lack of education or through insufficient mental capacity." [36] Contempt for the average worker is obvious, even as Taylor frosted it with paternalistic advice on how both worker and boss could prosper.

At best, even if a worker "had the necessary education and habits of generalizing in his thought, he lacks the time and the opportunity for developing these laws" of productive, efficient work.[37] Taylor was convinced that a craft economy was outmoded, that is, an economy in which everyone learns while working as an apprentice so that he understands the occupation and has a real opportunity to help improve its methods and tools. Assuming that greater productive power must give most of us less rather than more control over our lives, Taylor presumes that most employees will be consigned to routinized labor. An elite staff loyal to the corporation will break down work into jobs in a way that cheapens labor, the main element of cost.

Trying to routinize everything

The most well-known image of Taylorism is a man with a stopwatch conducting a so-called time-and-motion study on a worker. The stopwatch man is rare today, but the Taylorist crusade to remove judgment and skill from jobs continues, for example, in an attack on the elite occupation of physician.

Corporate and government experts demand that physicians follow so-called clinical practice guidelines. They want the physician to fill in data about a patient on a computer screen: her vital signs, yes/no checks about the presence or absence of this or that symptom, etc. Then the computer presents the guideline: prescribe this drug, perform this procedure, tell the patient to do this exercise.

The physician can press a key to accept the guideline, generating instructions for himself, nurses, and pharmacists. What if the physician disagrees with the guideline? With more or less difficulty he can override it, but then he must worry about whether he will be at greater risk of a malpractice charge, not to mention pressure from colleagues and managers. For example, a consortium of health insurers ranks Dr. Ann T. Nutt and other Massachusetts physicians. Her quality rank fell from Tier 1 to Tier 3 because she complied with guidelines only 115 out of 127 times. Nutt said she knew specific things about the twelve exceptional patients that led her to put proper care for them above toeing the line. All her patients will now have a higher copayment.[38]

Supposedly, the guidelines are "evidence-based," boiling all available scientific and clinical studies into their decision trees. One problem is who prepares the guidelines: the staff of health insurance corporations and other business-oriented operatives, usually with the help of a carefully selected physician.

More significantly, the success of the guidelines is decided on statistical results. The guidelines work in 95 percent of the cases, so they must be good. Too bad for the other five percent of patients who lose an organ, who are mangled for life, or die. Worse, the process is repeated in a cycle. Instead of widening successful outcomes by improving the clinical insight and judgment of all physicians, resources go into "improving" the guidelines behind the backs of most of them. The revised guidelines are bound to lose some patients, but again, if the 95 percent threshold is met, the guidelines must be good. Clinical practice guidelines reduce hands-on caregivers to mere followers of a treatment script. The loss of their experience and judgment means that care fails more often and the pool of wisdom in the caregiving occupations starts to evaporate. It is true that eventually a category of health failures and even mortality will become a major quantity in society, worthy of the same mechanical analysis, but only after much loss of life and lore.[39]

Computers are a great help in implementing restrictive guidelines. However, computer networks themselves are not the problem. On the contrary, it would be great if physicians were free to consult literature online rapidly while figuring out a course of action with the patient. Computers could also help physicians add their own notes that report and reflect on interesting cases.

There are ways to encourage physicians not to become set in their ways, to keep improving their "feel" and judgment, but they run directly counter to modern Taylorism, the corporate drive to confine everyone, even physicians, to routinized labor.

Instead, corporate experts prefer bonus payments and other incentives to promote health care by script. "Applying those guidelines in practice requires systems to structure the environment in which care is delivered so that 'doing the right thing' becomes automatic. This requires tools that simplify and provide focus by embedding the recommendations for evidenced-based care into the care itself. ... Clearly, appropriate financial incentives and regulatory stimuli can play a role."[40]

Few of us will ever become medical doctors, but many of us are treated by physicians at a critical moment. Health care is a growth sector of the economy, which signals to managers of corporatized medicine that potential cost savings are great if they can impose industrial labor not only on physicians, but on nurses and other caregivers who are pushed to follow clinical practice guidelines.

A similar campaign to degrade work to routinized labor is underway in the education "industry." It is based on giving students frequent tests using multiple choice and similar passive regurgitation. The goal is to make teachers teach to the tests by following scripts in lock step.

Success, then failure, of the industrial economy

For 200 years or so in the United States, England, and other pioneer countries of industrial capitalism, mechanization expanded social productive power. New industries appeared while old occupations faded away. Routinized labor was the basis of creating real wealth. The factory model extended into office work when corporations came to need as many workers for administrative chores as they required to make the products.

With enough united struggle workers won a share of the goods and services they created. They also won social benefits, including a gradual extension of universal education from public elementary school to high school. After World War Two a year or two of community college became common. Although four years of college were never proposed to be universal, science and engineering fields got a boost after the shock of Sputnik, the first satellite placed into space – by the Soviet Union in 1957, not the United States.

Then real wage growth stalled, entering a period of stagnation that continues to this day. With that turnaround, education changed, too. There are roughly three major parts to the change.

Decent elementary education for a huge part of the population is collapsing, especially in large cities. Children grow to be 18 years old, and written words and numbers remain semi-foreign objects. Reading for leisure, for understanding society, and for the sheer humanity of it are unknown to many. A sense of how quantities stand in proportion to each other, so that percentages convey useful information, for example, is rudimentary.

A second part of each generation acquires basic reading and arithmetic skills. Their aspiration to higher education as a way to economic advancement, however, is denied. Four years at a good college is simply too expensive.

Those youth who get to college find two big differences from what previous generations experienced. First, the cost of college has become enormous, rising about twice as fast as overall inflation over the last 30 years.[41] The family that is not rich simply cannot pay for it, even when the student works a reasonable number of hours. Instead, the student goes into debt, mortgaging a decade of work life to pay back loans – if there is still a job in his chosen field. Two out of three students graduate with debt, up from half of graduates in 1993. Their average burden is $19,000, twice what it was a decade earlier.[42]

Despite the greater financial strain for those who can afford four or more years to graduate from college, the economic reward is no better than it used to be. College for many is no more than a way to stay in place rather than fall lower on the economic ladder.[43]

More than ever, well-to-do families dominate in sending their children to elite colleges. They get training for truly lucrative careers, or they network their way into a winner's circle, or a combination of both.

Speedup modernized

The economy and education are not reinforcing each other to advance mass prosperity. Work is changing, but the essence of it is still industrial labor. It is a new form of speedup. A commission of businessmen and professors told a

70

fascinating combination of truths and lies about this change. They began a report:

"The premise is simple: Break complex jobs into a myriad of rote tasks, which the worker then repeats with machine-like efficiency. The system is managed by a small group of educated planners and supervisors."[44]

That is how the Commission on the Skills of the American Workforce described typical work in 1990. By this time it was clear to observers that things were changing. Employers pressed workers to remember more work processes and juggle lots of operations at once ("multitasking"). Inexpensive computers made it possible to deliver lots of information to employees, eliminating layers of middle managers and auxiliary staff as a bonus. Workers do not ponder the reports on their screens like scientists, coming up with new generalizations. Similarly, with the spread of cell phones, work conversations have become more frequent and hectic. Employees must react to bits and pieces of information with quick, tiny responses. The commission tried desperately to find an optimistic way out while retaining the existing economic order. Almost laughably, the commission tried to dress up the increased intensity: "Workers are asked to use judgment and make decisions. Management layers disappear as front-line workers assume responsibility for many of the tasks – from quality control to production scheduling – that others used to do."[45]

The assembly line job where you attach one part over and over is indeed almost gone. (However, this kind of work is kept alive in low-wage countries; we will discuss globalization later.) Still, most workers are not hired for a valuable skill like a registered nurse or an electrical engineer, who amount to exceptions in the economy. Nor is their work life a manager's advance up a ladder. Nor do most people move through a wide range of fuzzy staff positions, an avenue available to a few people with a generalized high-quality college education.

Recognizing the truth that front-line workers. are required to do more, the business commission then told the lie, "work organizations like these require large investments in training." Evidence in the rest of the report, however, documents how little training there is in the economy: "Only eight percent of our front-line workers receive any formal training once on the job, and this is usually limited to orientation for new hires or short courses on team building or safety."[46] The commission did not even try to show that there really are lots of workers asked to use judgment and that employers underwrite serious education for them.

The commission crowned its farce by recommending: "All employers will invest at least one percent of their payroll for the education and training of their workers."[47] In the polarized economy today, that means almost nothing for 90 percent of employees.

A genuine leap from industrial labor to skilled work – keeping in mind that judgment drawn from experience, knowledge and reflection is the key thing – requires overall understanding of the craft or science involved. Referring to a help screen or manual for a forgotten detail is not enough. Today we underrate apprenticeship and plain experience, but that is a great deal of what makes outstanding nurses and teachers, for example. They have learned by pondering experience with deep commitment to the mission, just what an employer does not want to pay for and depend on. The next step is to combine this knowledge with scientific understanding by the worker herself. Capitalism cannot take this step.

The end of squeezing riches out of industrial labor

Can economic development based on industrial labor go on forever? Two broad but conflicting trends show that it cannot.

On one hand science-based development of new technologies shows no end in sight. Machinery and automated production processes put science to work. Their powers keep expanding, able to transform materials in new ways. Machines carry out mechanical, chemical, and biological engineering processes. Furthermore, different processes are strung together with computerized management. Electronic sensors, computers, and robots can tell when to put the raw materials of plastic into a chemical vat; when to remove the liquid plastic, pipe it into molds, apply heat and measure until the stuff is properly baked; and when to remove the finished kitchen bowl, watch case, etc.

There is always more to learn about how nature works, which also means that our productive and transformative powers have no discernible expiration date.[48]

On the other hand, there definitely is a limit to what human muscle and nerve can do when they are used repetitively and with limited education. Although we can work longer and more intensely than people a century ago, although we are taller (and lately, fatter), we are basically the same physiological human beings we have been for thousands of years. There is also a limit to mental speedup, the multitasking demanded of workers today.

Every year machines have less need for the assisting eyes, ears, and hands of industrial labor. Humans seem unable to keep up because of their physiological limits, but the limits apply only because capitalism insists that most work must be industrial labor and most workers must be human machines. It is no surprise that machines based on advancing science finally push them aside.

The contradiction between the science-based power of machines and the limits of human beings used for industrial labor cannot be evaded. Socks and semiconductors pour out in torrents while more of the workforce is shown out the gate, abandoned by corporations and the political order, left to cheapen themselves for any replacement work they can get. No wonder wages lag far behind the increase in wealth.

For more than 200 years machines displaced workers. A new machine and the reduced number of workers who operated it produced things at a lower cost than the previous setup. Many people had to find new industrial jobs. The important thing is that the economy generated them. Workers were able, with a fight, to get wage increases from employers who were eager to get on with business. (This was on average over the ups and downs of prosperity and downturn.)

Increases in educational resources for each worker were gradual, and so were changes in the nature of work. Someone laid off from a coal mine did not need more than a few days of training to do a job on an automobile assembly line. There was time for the son of an assembly line worker to get a high school education and take an office job, and common people were able to get public education to prepare for work.

The era based on masses of semiskilled workers doing one then another kind of routinized labor is coming to an end before our eyes. Now the productive processes of new industries simply do not need many industrial workers. Machines have reduced the need for industrial labor to a tipping point. Common people can no longer maintain their share in the output and rewards of the economy.

The end of industrial labor applies throughout the economy, not only in manufacturing. Warehouses are automated to pull customer orders. The orders come from sales placed through an Internet website. Accounting is computerized, too.

To be sure, a science-fiction fantasy of total automation is not happening. The economy is not a complex of machines spitting things out for an idle population. What counts is that a specific form of work, industrial labor, is no longer at the heart of economic development.

When the automobile industry grew into the powerhouse of the economy in the first half of the twentieth century, millions of workers were drawn into assembly plants as well as feeder manufacturing of rubber tires, glass windshields, electrical parts, and so on. A new industrial Midwest arose.

All industries mature and level off. The auto vehicle industry reached its plateau by the end of the 1950s. A couple of decades later the semiconductor industry became the powerhouse of the economy, expanding output by leaps and bounds – but workers in chip fabrication and computer assembly were not at the center of things. Not that many industrial workers were needed, certainly not enough to populate a whole region like the Midwest. The work was higher up the skill ladder. Designing, producing, and using semiconductor electronics and computers needed electrical and computer engineers, but they were not a mass phenomenon.

Instead, capitalist progress forces lower wages on desperate people. That actually forestalls elimination of what is now subhuman labor. For example, robots are capable of washing floors and cleaning carpets in office buildings. They could replace armies of janitors, but their low wages make it uneconomic to buy the robots. Besides, these people would face the prospect of unemployment; the social order is blocked from moving all of us forward.

Hints of liberated work

Capitalism took craft mastery away from us. Carpenters have used tools like hammers for ages. The potentialities and requirements of production today demand a new order of work that uses modern instruments as craft tools.

To recover a secure, comfortable, and fulfilling life, we must devote more resources to assuring that common people, not only an elite, obtain both modern skills and an overview of society and its needs. Then they can use advanced machines with judgment and wisdom. However, it is exactly this leap to skilled and socially conscious work that capitalism cannot accept.

The development of productive powers is coming into unavoidable contradiction with the capitalist necessity to jigger work as industrial labor.

The circular orbit of viable capitalism was to make a profit and invest it in new machines, in whole new industries that took up the industrial labor released by rising productiveness in established industries. That circle has broken.

Automated new machines and processes based on the sciences crowd out industrial labor. Capitalist corporations cannot make money on millions of people whose developed skill is human work, broadly based in a high level of culture, education, and social understanding – all requiring broadly decided allocation of resources directly for human development. Such resources would be at the expense of profits that were invested in equipment and facilities. People cannot be owned like a machine. Except in small supplemental amounts, corporations cannot "invest in people," neither directly nor through toleration of taxes on their revenues and profits. The very phrase "invest in people" and its partner "human capital" express the contradiction that is the problem. Everyone knows that the returns on an investment go the investor.

Capitalism is not going to help us meet the challenge. There is no profit in it. On the contrary, corporate capital sees only social expense as well as a diminished role for profit and investment. The big powers of an economic order will not commit social suicide.

When machines become tools for workers, people will use them and participate in figuring out their best social use. While masses of everyday things pour out of automated plants, there is plenty of work for people to do in health care, education, customized construction, and activities we cannot even imagine yet. Work in those factories that are not automated will apply craft methods, use sophisticated tools, and manufacture customized products. With guaranteed full employment as a foundation, every job will be important because otherwise machines will do it.

Education of youth will awaken and develop talents we all have. On this broad foundation, people during a lifetime of human work will easily take a year or two to prepare for another occupation, do productive work for five or ten years (or longer if desired), then turn to a completely different kind of work, again with a year or two of preparation. We will become a society of uncommon common people. This is about doing socially useful work, not about attaching workers to machines.

We saw earlier that the major groups of the agrarian economy, the oligarchy of exploiters and the peasants, were under no compulsion to drive things forward to the end of the economic order. It is different with capitalism. Its economic compulsions have led it to push the productiveness of industrial labor forward. The process has now hit a brick wall, the contradiction between science-based productiveness and the limits of industrial labor. The existing economic order cannot resolve the dilemma.

Relentless grinding down

Until 1973 people were able to win wages that enabled them to purchase a stable share of our output. Most but not all enjoyed rising standard of living as new and affordable things became available. Since that year, real wages have stagnated and inequality has grown tremendously.

This trend, more than three decades long, is clearly entrenched in the economy, pushing common people down relentlessly.

• In 1973 families exactly in the middle of the income scale earned $42,825 (converted to 2003 dollar value), while a family in the top five percent earned $151,541. Bad enough, but after 30 years the middle family was only up to $53,016 – and working more hours to get it – while the five-percent family got $281,467.[49]

• Out of every 100 families in 1973, 80 of them earned 59 percent of all family income. Their share fell to 52 percent by 2005. Over the same period, the top five percent of families increased their take from 15½ percent to 21 percent.[50] In other words, most families lost, the top five percent took almost all the gain, and the 15 percent in the "upper middle" held onto about the same share.

• Families in the top one-tenth of one percent, who sit above 999 families out of 1000, increased their take of all income in the U.S. from 2 percent in 1973 to 7 percent in 2004.[51]

The biggest winners are the super-rich owners and chief executives of corporations, plus the wheeler-dealers in an increasingly speculative capitalism. They are supplemented by a small fraction of the people in selected occupations: a corner-cutting, well-connected elite among lawyers, accounting magicians, and other business professionals; marketing people lucky enough to ride fashionable trends; and some engineers and scientists in a hot field of the moment.

For 90 percent of the population, economic and social life has gotten worse. They suffer reduced living standards, greater risk of big disaster in their lives, more hours at work, and even more unsatisfying and exhausting jobs. Such has been the case since 1973, and there is no end in sight.

• Retirement security has turned into worry. Social Security, although it has never been large enough to ensure comfort, is guaranteed every month from retirement to death. Private pensions used to supplement Social Security in the same manner. These are called defined benefit plans. For decades, however, employers have substituted defined contribution accounts. You get a monthly deposit into an account; you may add part of your paycheck to it. Now it is your challenge to figure out how to keep the money for decades. If you leave it in a bank account, inflation will outpace the interest earned. When you "invest" in stocks, bonds, and other kinds of financial paper, well, your retirement funds can be slashed in half in a moment.

Although many employees in 1975 had no pension, three out of every four plans provided a stable defined benefit. By 2005 only one out of three was guaranteed. The rest of the private-employer retirement accounts were defined contribution plans.[52] Forced gambling in financial markets – glorified as workers becoming capitalists – turned out to be a rigged game. How can the common person, busy at work, outguess and outmaneuver Wall Street insiders who are at their trading terminals? The typical outcome has been the need to working five or ten years longer than you had been told would be necessary.

• Despite great leaps in scientific understanding of how our bodies work, health care is becoming a big problem for more people. People do not get the care that their parents more often got through the job. The government refuses to extend Medicare to everyone and guarantee equal care for all. We are blamed for our health problems while obvious sources of illness are ignored because the corporate interests of the rich would be affected. These untouchable social issues include industrial chemicals at work and in products, buildings, the air, and the water; obesity-causing food eaten as we rush through fast meals, while healthy food is a pricey luxury; and long hours of work that leave no time for restorative exercise and recreational leisure.

• Growing inequality turns off a social relief valve. Many oligarchs know it is smart to pluck a few youth from the common people and grease their way into high-income positions. This mobility has largely stopped. Resources are removed from public elementary and secondary schools precisely in the neighborhoods where the poor and middle live – because housing is segregated by income, too. The well-to-do nurture public schools in their neighborhoods with extra money, or they just send their children to private school. Then tuition and expenses for college present an even more unequal barrier. The annual charges at elite colleges are several times what most families earn, while a vocational course at a two-year college is never preparation for the 15 percent of jobs that are elite. From 1973 to 2005 the hourly wage in inflation-adjusted dollars declined for high school graduates, stayed basically the same for people who got a partial college education, and rose only for college graduates.[53]

• More people are pulled into the worst disasters of dire poverty. This is evident from statistics on income distribution. As long as there is any inequality, there will be 20 percent of families in the bottom fifth of the income rankings. That is by arithmetical definition. However, their average income compared to a family in the middle (the median) fell from 30 cents on the dollar in 1973 to 25½ cents in 2003.[54]

We are well on the way to becoming a country of the rich and everyone else. Federal income tax returns for 2006 that show adjusted gross incomes (AGI) of $1 up to $40,000 account for more than half of the returns filed, 79 million out of 138 million. Their total AGI was about the same as the total income of a mere 353,000 tax returns reporting AGI of $1 million or more.[55]

Taking the long historical view, the fourth economic period of human history based on Industrial labor is drawing to a close. The agrarian era persisted for thousands of years. After it cracked, capitalists demanded that they be allowed to buy and sell anything, and especially to hire workers. Once they won that fight, all of us were drawn into the vortex of an economic tornado. Capitalists found themselves caught up in imperatives of economic development at an increasing pace. They had no choice; capitalism is a system driven by economic laws.

After only about 500 years of capitalism, the barrier to its further development has appeared. The oligarchs will resist the coming era of liberated labor, and it will not happen without a great upheaval. But it is impossible the clock of history is ticking, and it is impossible to pull the hour hand back.

The program for common prosperity

The powers of machines, chemistry, electronics, and biology have eliminated the need for most routinized labor. Machines themselves do not degrade work; that is what happens when capitalists reduce most jobs to industrial labor.

We must solve the problem of work. The longer we wait, the worse things get for everyone except the rich.

The only solution for common people is to put *three basic principles* at the foundation of social life. Together they define the next economic regime, an egalitarian economic order.

• The first principle is to eliminate rich and poor. Abolish dividend, interest, and capital gains income derived from large private ownership. Then, over time, raise the wages of all jobs that pay below average, qualify people for improved jobs, and reduce the highest salaries.

We must converge toward wage equality. As long as some people are cheap labor, the business incentive to exploit industrial labor persists, carried out by slicing work into semiskilled and routine labor as a way of reducing production costs.

A lot can be done almost overnight to abolish deep poverty and obscene wealth, but full implementation of the no rich, no poor principle is the main economic and political task of several generations. It is a task of continual improvement in the work people are qualified for and actually do.

Hypocritical talk about the dignity of work has been paired with low wages and dirty, unsafe working conditions for ages. Humdrum labor and hard, dirty toil will not disappear, but the next economic order cannot allow large differences in wages. No rich, no poor has become an economic necessity, not an optional moral choice. Recognition of that necessity will bring genuine respect for all labor and every job. Honor for everyone who does his work with dedication becomes real because it goes with a good wage that is converging toward an equal wage.

• The second principle is the inalienable right to a job. Full employment is something we have known how to do since the 1930s.

Raising wages for the mass of employees increases the business incentive to automate labor. Full employment means there are always new jobs ready for people released from outmoded work.

• Third, we must change corporations, the main organizational units of the economy, into institutions of genuine economic service. Today

86

they are the wealth faucet of the rich. The principle is to convert them into organizations that produce and compete on a breakeven basis. The charter of corporations becomes a mandate that they shall make and sell goods and services without taking out profit, but also without incurring losses that drain society of resources.

A corporation that breaks even is doing fine. Any profit it makes goes to a social investment fund. A corporation that loses money for too long changes its managers or is reorganized, merged, or dissolved. Since every person who wants a job will have one, the changes can be worked out without mass suffering.[56]

One exception from the breakeven law for some time to come will be small business. People can start a business and grow it, but when it reaches a threshold (perhaps around the level today at which big corporations buy out family businesses), the regular rules of the egalitarian order must go into effect. Some service and niche craft businesses are difficult to organize on a large scale. This exception also provides an outlet for the determined person who is set on a project but cannot find a corporation or institution that will fund it and let him carry it out.

The principle of economic service for corporations means the end of getting rich by owning stock and collecting dividends. People will not own stock. (Social Security will be doubled, giving security to the average retired person, so we can shut down the rigged 401(k) game in which busy working people are fleeced by full-time speculators and multi-billion dollar hedge funds.)

These three principles — no rich, no poor; jobs for all as a basic right; and chartering corporations for economic service — open the way for all of us together to produce the things and provide the services that we need and want. We will enjoy them in a new mass prosperity.

Economic equality cannot be done by handouts. It is not a program of taxing the rich and dispensing a dole to the poor. The no rich, no poor program introduces an era of transforming society, culture, and individual lives. The theoretical end of this program is that all jobs pay the same – a task of several generations.

And make no mistake, we must be serious about social equality. Every able person has work; income gaps narrow to the point that there are no longer some who are rich and others who are poor. If any sizeable number of people were left behind, pressure to use them at cheaper wages would undermine the whole program and open the way for a return to the mess we are in today.

Young adults might start at a lower rate with automatic increases for every year of work. By middle age everyone would be earning well above $72,000 a year. Whatever the life cycle, it would apply to everyone.

Inequality today has become so extreme that we can level up nearly everyone, not level down.

88

A few multi-billion dollar families will no longer receive outrageous incomes. After that, economic justice can be achieved in good part by raising below-average incomes with the gains of productiveness. Incidentally, the ten percent today who enjoy income privilege can bear a cap on their incomes. They will have good food and a warm home. Most will even learn to enjoy life in the new society.

The egalitarian economic order will overhaul the division of work. Say goodbye to the business principle of dumbing down jobs. Just the opposite, the demand on society will be to minimize such labor, educating each generation of workers to a uniform and higher standard of capability, being productive not by wearing oneself out at a machine or keyboard but by using equipment and scientific processes as the tools of new crafts.

Role of education

As we implement the no rich, no poor program, education will become a real avenue of progress. A business executive, Richard Elkus, spent the last four decades of the twentieth century in electronics and semiconductor corporations. He watched United States engineers develop digital electronics from the videotape recorder to cell phones, only to see companies let the new industries move offshore. He went looking for answers. What is the place of education? Elkus described how schools fit into a capitalist economy:

"The education system is not a leading indicator of national competitiveness but a lagging indicator. It reflects rather than anticipates the national vision. It will not succeed any better than the economic and political system it is designed to support. ... Simply put, students study and teachers teach subjects related to where the jobs are. If there is no demand for a particular expertise, there is little incentive for either students or teachers to invest their time in it."[57]

Elkus is largely correct. The usual objection to blunt statements like his is a lament that schools should give students a broad foundation of general knowledge. They should develop critical thinking, independent judgment, appreciation for good writing, drawing, and music, and so on. Yes, a privileged few can focus on these liberal arts, but the business executive is correct in saying that mass education meets economic requirements first. The development of an alert, active, sensitive human being is confined to leftover time.

There is one exception. A college education in humanities like history and literature can be a ticket to a niche of good jobs in corporations, government, and grant-funded agencies. Some executives recognize that it helps to keep a handful of people around with intellectual depth. Sufficient knowledge of technicalities can be acquired quickly. The ambitious graduate must, of course, apply his capacities to the specific mission of the organization.

Elkus's observation that schools are largely confined to an economic function has more bite when we hear it from a pompous member of the oligarchy. In 1909 Woodrow Wilson was president of Princeton University; in eight years he would be president of the country. Wilson said in a speech to high school teachers:

"We want one class to have a liberal education. We want another class, a very much larger class of necessity, to forego the privilege of a liberal education and fit themselves to perform specific difficult manual tasks."[58]

Most jobs in the early twentieth century were divided into a few manual tasks by corporate design, following the advice of Frederick Taylor. Even engineers prepared for their jobs by vocational training embroidered with slight trimmings of liberal education. Businessmen did not need higher education; when they attended college, their purpose was to enter social networks and acquire a few manners of elevated status.

Still, Wilson's statement outrages us. For one thing, it bluntly calls liberal education a privilege. More important, Wilson makes it clear that the oligarchy does not want to develop the economy in a direction that requires mass liberating education, including an overview of history, appreciation of reason as a broad outlook not merely a specialized tool, and the unleashing of urges to do something worthwhile in this world. Instead, the oligarchy confines economic development for as long as possible to technological advance without human progress. So long as there was a minimum of mass prosperity, the oligarchy got its way. Now that we have reached the barrier to proceeding along this road, the time has arrived for a new economic order and, as a requirement of it, a new educational system.

The no rich, no poor economic program lays down requirements for a new education system. Schools will need to qualify an ever wider majority of people for good jobs because more and more positions will become good jobs. When the new commonwealth publishes a schedule of a rising minimum wage, coming closer all the time to the average wage, you can be sure employers will insist on schools that provide more capable employees. Since the big gaps in family incomes will be going away, so too will shortfalls in the financing and performance of schools. Furthermore, when the economy serves common people and they get involved in running corporations and the rest of society, the need and urge for liberated education will be felt and satisfied – education built on the tradition of the liberal arts but with deep respect for work, the essential human activity.

The principles of the no rich, no poor program imply similar changes in health care, housing and neighborhoods, crime reduction, the uses of science, and more.

We had to review labor through all human history to realize why things cannot go on as they are and discover the way out to prosperous equality. Either we fight to the end for a system of no rich, no poor, or we bow to growing inequality and a declining standard of life for 90 percent of the population. Together the three principles define an egalitarian economic order. We were imagining it at the beginning of this essay:

If we took all the personal income in this country and paid it equally to everyone who wants a job, each of us would earn $72,000 a year for a full-time job. And by the way, there is enough left over to double all Social Security payments, too.

It was easy enough to make a hypothetical calculation, although almost no one has hammered on this statistic. Now we see that convergence toward wage equality is more than an exercise of arithmetic. It is the first principle of a new commonwealth.

Globalization

The pressure of jobs moving to cheap-labor countries is often identified as the reason for income losses of working people in the United States. It is a cause, but not the fundamental one.

Some experts deny there is any real problem with globalization. For them, the more global trade and investment, the better for everyone.

Almost always, though, the payoff for most people lies in the future. You need to change your occupation first. Maybe you have to do it on your own, or maybe some programs will help you.

Still, dangling a carrot in front of us is not very convincing these days. Manufacturing workers heard the lecture twenty years ago when the production of television sets and clothing went overseas. More people lost out when jobs at call centers and in bookkeeping and other data entry went overseas, and they heard the same advice. Now accountants and computer programmers are tossed aside with the same lecture while corporations send their work overseas by satellite and fiber optic cable.

The work moves downhill to lower-wage countries. Isn't it obvious that globalization is the cause of lower wages and longer hours forced on employees in the United States? Actually, it is not. Closer analysis does not deny common sense, but it sorts out cause and effect. Globalization, especially the outsourcing of jobs by corporations to lower-wage countries, is itself one result of the maturing contradiction of industrial labor in the United States, Europe, and Japan.

The turning point for routinized labor was 1973. The last wave of mass prosperity after World War Two was over by then. Ever since, incomes have stagnated and working hours and conditions have gotten worse, except for the rich. The big surge in the global export of jobs, however, did not get underway for a decade or more after 1973. Globalization that became significant ten years after decline set in cannot be the cause.

In the late 1970s Japan knocked out some important manufacturing sectors in the United States. Toyota took the crown of the automobile industry from the Big Three of Detroit. Leadership in television and other consumer electronics went to Sony, Panasonic and other Japanese corporations. These changes were not primarily based on wage differences between Japan and the United States.

In the 1980s assembly labor in electronics and shoes grew in southeast Asian countries like Malaysia and the Philippines. Still, the real tidal wave of job loss and wage pressure crashed on us later, around 1990. That is when U.S. corporations obtained access to low-wage workers in Russia and east European countries following the collapse of the Soviet Union.

Most importantly, the 1990s are when corporations moved into China in a big way. In 1990 urban manufacturing jobs in Chinese private firms (not owned by the state or collectives) were just over one million. Twelve years later the number was more than 15 million jobs.[59]

"The country's official data showed 83 million manufacturing employees in 2002, but that figure is likely to be understated; the actual number was probably closer to 109 million. By contrast, in 2002, the Group of Seven (G7) major industrialized countries had a total of 53 million manufacturing workers."[60]

Although manufacturing jobs left the United States for cheap-wage countries, the worldwide trend of eliminating manufacturing jobs is just as real, too. Economists compiled one study examining "employment trends in 20 large economies and found that from 1995 to 2002, more than 22 million jobs in the manufacturing sector were eliminated, a decline of more than 11 percent." Brazil had a 20 percent decline, and the total in China was down 15 percent.[61]

Increasing productiveness of machinery is nothing new. The problem is that nowhere in the world are tens of millions of better jobs being created. Instead, we also see corporations cutting labor costs in call centers and information processing by moving their jobs, too – to India, for example.

Mass prosperity in the United States passed its high mark in 1973, but global outsourcing became a big part of the picture only around 1990. The contradiction that brought an end to mass prosperity helps explain the spread of globalization.

For a century before 1973 the ruling powers of developed countries stifled industrial development in Asia, Latin America, and Africa. Most Third World countries were known for a single raw material export. In 1950 petroleum accounted for over 90% of Venezuela's exports, employing only 2% of the labor force.[62] Other countries mainly supplied a single crop or ore, too (Salvador: coffee; Egypt: cotton; Gambia: peanuts; Bolivia: tin; Hawaii: sugar and pineapples). Capitalists of the developed countries did not want industrial competition. They invested in the development of their own mass production, which they kept in the United States and western Europe.

Now global corporations of the U.S., Japan, and Europe figure they can keep advanced technology in their hands while they move production to cheap-wage countries. They enforce a global wave of leveling down.

It remains to be seen whether new capitalist regimes in China and Russia along with ambitious rulers in other low-wage countries can muscle their way into the world economic elite. It is a secondary question. All these big businessmen are running into the limit that capitalism has reached.

The political implications are clear. Our gut opposition to the institutions of globalization is correct. The North American Free Trade Agreement (NAFTA) has hurt common people in the U.S. and brought misery to Mexico's masses, too. It should be torn up. Similarly for the World Trade Organization (WTO). Expert economists shrink in horror at such demands. They raise the scarecrow of protectionism, the alleged folly of losing the benefits of world trade. They are wrong. World trade does not need to be conducted as global shifting of production, low-wage competition, and leveling down of all common people for the benefit of a handful of global rich.

An egalitarian economic order in the United States will be open to world trade, using it as an assist to domestic economic progress. Countries with more of a certain raw material than they can use need to sell them or at least sell semi-finished goods made from them. That is one basis for legitimate trade. There are others, but trade can and must be balanced and mutually beneficial.

Can the United States prosper without a flood of products made by cheap labor abroad? It is a legitimate question, considering that imports of goods rose from 9 percent of U.S. gross economic product in 1990 to more than 14 percent in 2007. Of course, the United States also exports. Weighing them in, the net deficit (imports of goods versus exports) rose from 2 percent of gross product in 1990 to 6 percent in 2007.

We used to make much of what is now imported. We can reclaim the manufacturing that left the U.S. economy. The wages of U.S. employees in an egalitarian economic order will be much higher than the low wages on which globalization feeds. That means production in the United States will be more automated than it is under globalization. When production wages rise, the incentive to automate increases. It can and will be done. Athletic shoes are assembled today by low-wage workers in the Philippines, Vietnam, China and so on. When shoe producers must pay an egalitarian wage in the U.S. and are not allowed to move the industry to cheap-wage countries, they will find ways to assemble shoes with much less labor. Automation is also no problem for U.S. employees when a new and better job is available, with social support for the required education, because full employment is a bedrock principle of society.

A new commonwealth in the United States will be happy to help sister regimes. When we have a vigorous economy at home, we welcome peaceful development in other countries. Among other benefits, progress in these countries, by relieving the economic desperation of their people, will take steam out of immigration into the United States.

Reactionary commentators blame global wage competition for our woes, often with a dollop of accurate facts, but they are demagogues. They promote a mindless "we're number one!" diversion, insisting that the United States must dominate the world.

On the other hand there is an elitist show of sympathy for the masses of the Third World. Somehow, the common people of the United States are supposed to regard our economic achievement with guilt. Nonsense. Behind the crocodile tears of the rich at the plight of immigrants is a business mind calculating how to take advantage of cheap labor. Equality cannot be achieved by leveling down.

Economic equality is not a timeless moral ideal. The moment has arrived for a regime in the United States founded on the principles of economic equality. Distinct countries are still a reality of this world, and the common people of each one must find their own way. A new commonwealth in the United States will be a friend ready to give economic and technical aid to other countries for the purpose of joining a new era.

Beyond the New Deal

The Great Depression of the 1930s in the United States (and most of Europe) threw tens of millions of people into desperate situations. A quarter of all workers had no job. Many people did not know where they would get their next meal. In 1932 New York City scheduled 37,000 evictions a month. A year later half of all home mortgages were in default; one in ten went into foreclosure.[63]

The country flipped from the Jazz Age frivolities of the 1920s to protests, demands for relief, and widening sentiment for an end to capitalism. Discontent brought results in the New Deal, which turned out to be the high point of economic reform in United States history.

The federal government provided some relief and jobs. Unemployment benefits were created. So was Social Security for retired people. Significant minimum wage laws, rules on overtime and other fair labor practices were enacted. Financial markets were regulated.

Most important, the government and corporate employers conceded workers the right to organize unions. It was a right on paper, and making it real was not automatic. Workers had to fight corporations one after another to get their industrial unions. The unions were called industrial, not only because many of them were situated in mass production of automobiles, rubber, steel, and electrical appliances, but also because these unions enrolled all employees in a factory from the assembly line workers to the skilled machinists and other craftsmen. Previously unions confined themselves almost entirely to narrow groups of skilled craft workers. At last, the people who performed industrial labor were united in organizations that could face the employer on a more nearly level field.

The labor shortages generated during World War Two enabled organized workers to consolidate and extend their gains, and nearly half of all war veterans went to college on the GI Bill.[64]

In Europe, workers had not only unions but also political parties and a deeper sense of "us" versus "them." They won more of their gains in the form of government plans for social welfare, while in the United States benefits were typically bargained in contracts with employers. This difference had a big impact in health care. European countries guarantee care through plans that cover nearly the entire population, while in the United States health plans were negotiated in contracts with individual employers. Not until the 1960s would the U.S. government enact Medicare for people over 65. As of 2009, 47 million people are still left out, mostly people working for employers who offer no health plan, or plans too expensive for all but their top staff.

Although industrial unions achieved some power to bargain over the speed of assembly lines and the wage differentials paid for different job titles, unions made virtually no dent in the employers' power to carve work into semiskilled, routinized jobs.

President Franklin D. Roosevelt saved capitalism in the United States by conceding just enough to keep common people from getting serious about an alternative economic system. Reluctantly, capitalist oligarchs accepted unions and social programs that put a few restraints on the raw job market. However, a sizeable fraction of big businessmen were unwilling to make any concessions. Some of them, including Duponts and Morgans, plotted to overthrow Roosevelt. In 1933 they offered a recently retired Marine general, Smedley Butler, enough money to assemble an army and take over Washington, D.C. He refused to do it.

While a Great Depression ravaged the industrialized United States and Europe, the Soviet Union was a stark contrast. The common people there had risen up during the mass suffering of World War One, 1914-1918, overthrown the czar, and entrusted power to a party of uncompromising workers, the Bolsheviks. By the 1930s the Soviet Union was industrializing without economic depression. Instead, prosperity was steady while workers enjoyed shorter hours until just before World War Two. (It is a lesson in the elastic meaning of emotional labels that the communist party in China pursues an opposite path today, one of hiring out the national labor force to multinational corporations at cheap wages. Unemployment in China jumped up by millions when the worldwide crash of 2008 hit.)

President Roosevelt was able to find a capitalist way out, and the working class was able to win unions and reforms without turning to a new economic system. The postwar years from 1945 to 1973 were the last era of mass prosperity under capitalism. It was based on job growth in two opposite directions, one heading toward an economic order beyond industrial labor and the other embodying the decay of capitalism. The split trend is shown in employment by industry in 1950 and 1970. During these two decades manufacturing shrank from 34 to 28 percent of all nonfarm jobs. Indeed, a few years later in 1979, manufacturing topped out at 21 million jobs. Despite a much larger workforce as of 2008, there are only 13 million manufacturing jobs.

Job growth was in services and government. Services went from 12 percent of all nonfarm jobs in 1950 to 16 percent in 1970, then to 25 percent by 1990. However, the growth of service jobs was divided fairly evenly between two kinds. One group of services heralds a new economic order surpassing industrial labor: education, health, and some professional services to Industry. Growth of government, especially in education, took it from 13 percent of jobs in 1950 to 18 percent in 1970, but government employment has only fluctuated since then. Other services are features of ornate decay: law, accounting, office temp agencies, and leisure and hospitality.[65]

The social welfare programs and union strength won in the 1930s and 1940s eroded. Real wages stagnated. Families had to provide more hours to employers (both husband and wife, or two partners, and often the teenage children, too) in order to keep up. For awhile, more education was the way out, at least for 15 to 20 percent of the workforce, but governments are running public elementary education into the ground and turning it over to private operators, while raising the tuition and fees of higher education.

The New Deal of the 1930s is being dismantled. The government bureaucratic machinery that accepted unions now prevents workers from organizing one. Unemployment insurance, workers' compensation, programs to find a viable new occupation when old jobs disappear, programs of housing construction, and on and on are whittled down into cheap caricatures of their glory days.

The first steps to be taken by a new commonwealth are familiar because they will likely renew the programs of the New Deal and extend them. With the recognition that building an egalitarian economy is a project of several generations, a high minimum wage that a worker and his or her children can really live on is a beginning. So, too, are social programs to deliver the modern basics that are vital but so expensive now: good education; guaranteed health care; and security in retirement (with humane opportunities for seniors to work).

Where will the money for these measures come from? The first phase of the no rich, no poor program can easily chop down the income of the tiny one percent or less at the top. These few receive most of their income from owning stocks, bonds, and such, as well as obscene corporate salaries and bonuses. The rich will live just fine even after we take most of it back.

About ten to fifteen percent of employees get more than the level of an equal wage. Many of them are managers and professionals who get two, three, or four times as much. In the first phase there will be an end to annual increases that are above average, but it is not necessary to reduce the incomes of these people. Some of them will warm up to the new regime because they will appreciate the vast changes for the better in society: the disappearance of homeless beggars on the streets; new energy in workplaces that serve the public good instead of distorting all activity for the maximum return to capital.

We can develop the talents in our children while they are young and continue through their lives so that we finally raise a generation who make the equal wage a natural feature of the economy, building momentum to grow on its own accomplishments.

The mission of the New Deal was to save capitalist property (most of it had long since become corporate property) and salvage the regime of industrial labor. The new commonwealth is about prosperity for all and developing human talent. The difference goes down to the foundations of political rule.

The fundamental difference between the New Deal and the egalitarian economy, even at its beginning, is who rules and to what ends. Development and investments cannot be the province of the rich, the private owners and claimants of wealth and income. The principles of economic life must be changed. Only a regime committed to the no rich, no poor program can do that.

Conservatives, reformists, and the common people

The existing economic order grinds away, pushing down everyone except the richest few. What can we do about it? As soon as this question arises, we are led to sort out politics – the arena of conscious deliberation about society, but also the realm of institutional power.

Because there are many conflicting economic interests in a capitalist society, they generate innumerable political conflicts, large and small. Looking at the big issues, all positions sort into three distinct stands about what must be done.

1) Conservatives, using myths about the economy against its realities, demand that we keep our hands off "the market."

2) Reformists promise that the existing order can be improved for the benefit of everyone, even while the rich keep their riches.

3) Only the no rich, no poor program serves the needs of common people.

Conservatives

Conservatives deny that the economic order has a basic problem. Just accept whatever the free market wants to do and things will work out the best that any economic arrangement can. You will waste resources and get worse results by trying to interfere with the sacred operation of markets.

If you want to get lost in an elaborate theory underlying these conclusions, the conservatives have it for you. An outstanding feature is that it allows no real history. Humankind stumbled along until a few societies discovered the magic answer for all time: unrestrained capitalism, also called the free market. While the life situation of an increasing majority gets worse, conservatives insist that human action would only make things worse.

Conservatives preach no interference whenever it would benefit common people, but they support plenty of meddling in favor of this or that group among the rich. Professor Milton Friedman, an ideologue of free-market capitalism, got caught in this contradiction. In 2003 Congress added a pharmaceutical drug benefit to the Medicare program. At the bidding of drug corporations, a provision in Part D makes it illegal for U.S. residents to buy drugs from Canada or any other country. Nor will the FDA arrange to inspect and certify the safety of imports. At first Friedman opposed the import ban. After all, free-market ideology says a buyer should be able to search anywhere for the best price. This stand outraged the pharmaceutical corporations. They have elaborate schemes by which they charge different prices for the same drug in different countries, depending on what they can get away with. Sure enough, Friedman dutifully reconsidered and came up with an elaborate excuse for the ban on buying drugs from Canada.[66]

In other words, markets must be free from rules that protect the interest of common people. Rules that resolve clashes between different capitalists are fine, thank you – although things are often not done by the book. Capitalism is full of conflicts resolved by payoffs and power as much as by a so-called rule of law.

Clashes between particular interests can be contained without becoming explosive, except when the particular interest is the universal interest of common people. For example, the law has almost always made it difficult and even impossible for groups of employees to bargain with employers in the job market. A big exception occurred in the 1930s when millions of workers were driven to desperation. They united, organized, and put their livelihood and their lives on the line simply to get a union and a negotiated contract. The rulers of capitalism had a choice. They could tear away the rule of law and move to crush the movement, as the German industrial magnates and bankers did by bringing in the Nazis, or they could recognize legal rights for workers' unions. The rulers of capitalism chose the latter course in the United States (although some big business interests preferred fascism, as we saw earlier). The National Labor Relations Act was passed and, after more fierce struggle by workers, implemented – for a few years. The legal field of action allowed to employees shrank with the passage of the Taft-Hartley Act in 1947. Ever since then it has become more difficult for workers to sign up with a union and negotiate a contract on pay and working conditions.

The conservatives, denying there is a real problem, have no program except rolling back whatever modest restraints have been imposed on the powers of big money.

Reformists

Reformists accept capitalism, but they understand that some modification of free markets is necessary for its political survival. They claim that the rich and the rest of us can all benefit from various regulations and programs.

When it comes to a program and the power to carry it out, reformists fall into two groups, liberals and social democrats.

Liberals admit they support continued existence of the rich and capitalism, although sometimes you have to press them. They might try to tell you, against all evidence, that we need not have poor people while there are rich persons. Or that the important thing is to reduce the number of poor as much as possible. Liberals keep within the political rules of the existing order. They believe not in the conservatives' credo – leave all power with the rich and step aside – but rather that the rich can be persuaded to grant a slice of power to reformers.

Unlike liberals, social democrats claim to be in favor a new economic order. Sooner or later, though, it becomes apparent they are really liberals. They believe a slice of power for the people is sufficient. With it they think they can introduce so many reforms that capitalism becomes something else, sometimes called socialism.

Directly addressing unequal incomes, a study by the experts of the International Labour Organization (ILO) summarized the reformist philosophy in a single paragraph. They begin, "Rising income inequality can be a good thing to the extent that it is crucial to reward work effort, talent and innovation – key engines of economic growth and wealth creation."[67]

Unequal incomes are crucial to reward effort? Albert Einstein did not concentrate his talent on the mysteries of the universe in order to become rich. The engineers and technicians who put the first man on the moon in 1969 did not enlist onto a great team because they wanted to become rich. Johann Sebastian Bach did not write some of the greatest music ever composed in order to get rich selling musical scores (the CDs of the 1700s). Outstanding teachers in schools across the country do not bring children to literacy, math understanding, and a love of literature, science, and music because they want to become rich.

There are many ways to reward effort, talent and innovation without promoting worship of riches. For example, prizes are an effective way to give honor and a one-time bonus for an outstanding achievement. Probably the most important reward for good work in the new commonwealth is more choice over how you develop your talent. Devote yourself to five or ten years of good performance where society needs it, and you earn the right to start a career in another field, including time off for free education to get ready. If you prefer to contribute more in your current field, that is your option, too.

We all need to know our basic needs will be met. Some people coming from a childhood of poverty spend their lives accumulating a mountain of wealth, clawing past everyone who deals with them. They vow they will never again worry about their next meal, but no matter how high they rise on a list of the richest persons in the world, they never have enough. Whether making more money in ever bolder looting or dissipating themselves in tawdry luxury, their poverty is that they have nothing inside. Money is the only measure of their worth that they can find.

As for those who come from wealthy backgrounds, they simply consider it their birthright to get more than almost everyone else.

Now that hunger, homelessness, and unemployment must become relics of history just like human sacrifice on burning pyres, it is time to develop more human ways of rewarding work. When we see that work is part of a social enterprise increasing everyone's comforts and encouragement to live a good life, the important reward for special effort will be new opportunities to realize your potential – not invidious wealth that adds little to real leisure.

So much for the new commonwealth. Let us get back to the good reformists at the ILO. While making it clear they favor inequality of income forever, the experts criticized "too much" inequality: "However, there are instances where income inequality reaches excessive levels, in that it represents a danger to social stability while also going against economic efficiency considerations. Indeed, higher income inequality is associated with higher crime rates and lower life expectancy."[68]

Reformist fear of common people

Social stability – that is the key to reformists. The ILO worries because the gap between the rich and common people leaves capitalism open to a political risk: "More fundamentally, when income inequalities are perceived to reach excessive levels, social support for pro-growth policies may be strongly eroded. Already now, there are widespread perceptions in many countries that globalization does not work to the advantage of the majority of the population."

Reformist Robert Reich said it even more plainly with a candid defense of incomes that are unequal but not too unequal. He explained that a huge gap between rich and the rest of us invites an upheaval that could do away with capitalism, and he certainly does not want that. The message was in a 2005 talk by Reich, "How Unequal Can America Get Before We Snap?" He presented statistics illustrating how wide the polarization of income and wealth has become. However, he did not calculate what the average full-time job would pay if all income were earned on a job and all jobs paid the same – $72,000 a year.

The snap in Reich's talk is the snap of a rubber band. He suggested that increasing the spread between the rich and the great majority is like stretching a rubber band:

"It either can snap back: you pull it elastically to such an extent, eventually it reaches such a point of extreme expansion that it just necessarily – you lose control, and it just snaps back. Or else, what happens to elastic bands when they get stretched? They could break. ... You can't just keep on going the way we are in terms of wealth and income inequality and also inequality of opportunity without some sort of snap back or snap break, at some point."[69]

Snapping back means reforms that shrink the spread between rich and the great majority. But what is "snap break," Reich's awkward phrase for a different solution to intolerably unequal incomes? Reich sees a terrible thing:

"The working class that we used to call it, and the poor, will increasingly become vulnerable to demagogues who come along and take their frustration and their anxiety and turn it into and divert it toward targets of animosity. We have seen this before in history. I don't have to tell you. We've seen it a little in the United States, not much, but we have seen angry populism. We saw it in the 1890s. The predecessor of Progressivism was populism. William Jennings Bryan, prairie populism. It was an angry populism. It was an angry, divisive populism. It was an angry, divisive populism that blamed a lot of people, some of them who were scapegoats for that populism. ... The politics of resentment is carried upon and depends upon anxiety and frustration, and is utilized by demagogues to further their own selfish purposes."[70]

Reich hates political action by common people. The good folks in the elite should take care of things, people like Reich himself; Bill Clinton, the president he served as secretary of labor; and now Barack Obama, the president whom Reich served as economic advisor; and the corporate elite behind all these public figures. They must reduce inequality of income a bit (snap back), or else common people might take over (break more than a rubber band) and proceed to implement the program of no rich, no poor.

115

Reich does not describe the inspiring common people's upsurge at the end of the nineteenth century. Instead, he reminds his audience of "populism," and when he brings it up, he concentrates on racial divisiveness and similar hatreds. Racism was indeed one strand of populism, although behind the Ku Klux Klan was the county sheriff, behind him were local political bosses, and behind them were the plantation owners, cotton merchants, and other economic powers. Reich, though, baits anyone who does not let him and the rest of the "good" elite solve the problem with reforms.

Social democrats parrot liberal Reich's warning that capitalism must curb the most outrageous inequality in order to survive. For example, Kevin Rudd was prime minister of Australia when the economic collapse of 2008 hit the country. He wrote:

"Not for the first time in history, the international challenge for social democrats is to save capitalism from itself: to recognize the great strengths of open, competitive markets while rejecting the extreme capitalism and unrestrained greed that have perverted so much of the global financial system in recent times."[71]

Rudd's praise of competitive markets is a straw man. A new commonwealth can have markets where companies required to operate on a breakeven basis compete for market share. The difference is that these firms will not pay dividends, will not reward stock market players, will not write multi-million dollar paychecks to executives, and will not determine the fate of society by private investments. The real point for social democrat Rudd, like liberal Reich, is to take a bit of the edge off the squeeze on common people. Both endorse greed but not extreme greed.

Rudd worries, "There is a grave danger that new political voices of the extreme Left and the nationalist Right will begin to achieve a legitimacy hitherto denied them." Rudd slaps derogatory labels on the real center of society, the common people who just want work, comfort, and genuine avenues of fulfillment.

Reformism does not refer to this or that demand for reform. Reforms are good: a progressive tax system that makes the rich pay more than most because they can and should pay more; universal health treatment on the principle of equal care for all; and laws with teeth that allow workers to organize into unions without intimidation by the employer. As one of those populists of the late nineteenth century, Mary Ellen Lease, put it, common people (farmers in her audiences) should "raise less corn and more hell" for reforms. If we win, that is a material and confidence-building victory. If we do not win, more people are open to seeing that the United States must have a new order of no rich, no poor.

Reformism should not be confused with fighting for a reform. Reformists fear an end to capitalism. Reformism is a warning to conservatives that they must not let that economic rape of the common people called the free market go on and on until the people decide to get rid of it all.

There was a time when Reich's plea for curbing extreme plunder by the rich and providing relief to the poor was a feasible program. That was when capitalism had not reached the end of prosperity built on industrial labor. The reforms of the Progressive Era at the beginning of the twentieth century took a little steam out of the upsurge of working people, but only for awhile. Inequality became even more extreme in the 1920s, and capitalism came near collapse in the Great Depression of the 1930s. More vigorous reforms were required to subdue the revolts of working people facing unemployment of 25 percent, mass evictions and foreclosures; farmers who could get no net income out of farming; and old folks who had no social security. The New Deal dangled enough hope with a bit of federal intervention and regulation of the economy. By the time of World War Two capitalism was back on its feet, this time until 1973.

Thirty-five years later no such revival of a workable economy is in sight. Reich's rubber band has stretched more than ever before. Capitalism has run into a barrier to mass prosperity that it cannot overcome. So what program do reformists like Robert Reich offer? They want many of the same things that are on the right-away list of an egalitarian order, but they want them under capitalism.

118

It can no longer happen that way.

Today the main contribution of Reich, of liberals and social-democrats and all reformists, is a negative one. Everything they tell common people amounts to admonishing them that on no account must they install their own social order in place of capitalism.

In Reich's case the recipe is, help the good part of the elite get a slice of power. We promise that we will exercise it in the interest of common people.

Other reformists tell the people that they can exercise their strength within the existing social order. They talk about building a tremendous movement. They even hug and puff about the threat of toppling the existing order if popular demands are not met. Really, though, they flatter common people that you can make Congress do your will; that no Supreme Court would dare nullify your laws; that federal marshals will execute your orders; that the police will hunt down terror gangs financed by wealthy reactionaries; that the National Guard will attend your mass demonstrations simply to protect them; and on and on with elaborate but ridiculous fantasies. The reformists' game plans combine boasting about an irresistible power of the people with a slavish devotion to preserving the existing economic order even as it is modified a bit.

A new commonwealth requires a new political order

The essence of a society is found in its relations of labor: institutions that grant producers access to the resources and equipment required for production; rights to possession of the product as soon as it is produced; and secondary relationships of authority at work.

There is also a set of institutions through which a society – or the ruling class in societies divided into a few rich and the great majority – coordinates conscious reflection and action on social issues, especially fundamental economic ones. Most important, the institutions include official bodies of force that compel obedience to the decisions made.

Today these institutions include:

• the government, where the bulk of the military and police bodies exist; also, deliberative, administrative, and judicial institutions,

• the media, which publish reports, stories, arguments, and opinions to society as a whole or to large chunks of it, and

• political parties and a host of other organizations that advocate one or another social action.

We may call this set of institutions the political realm. Politics in the large sense is the name for the social sphere that deliberates on and takes action in the name of society, backed up by coercion when necessary. (In a smaller sense, politics means hypocritical, dirty dealing by public officials. There is plenty of that, but we need a word for the larger sense, and politics is the traditional name.)

Together the political institutions operate as a "realm," a word that goes back to the Latin words *regimen*, meaning to control, and *regere*, to direct.[72]

Politics is not just discussing things and what to do about them. To be blunt, we must figure out the political realm because that is where the power is, the power to do something about the economic order. "Power consists, after all, in having the ability to ensure that others are prepared to do what you want them to do. ... people obey because they want to, or because they are afraid not to, or because they are forcibly compelled" to obey.[73] So says an extreme conservative in a book about the most conservative cities and groups in ancient Greece. (When it comes down to power, conservatives are usually more candid than reformists.)

Some people want to do one thing, other people want to do something else, and the clash of interests reveals which side has the power.

In societies afflicted with exploitation, a small group of rich basically controls the political realm. This is true when it comes to exercising power that affects the economic order, and most especially in maintaining the fundamental labor relations.

Not all the rich devote themselves to governing. A few of them do the actual ruling. The rich also cultivate and hire trusted agents to govern. They may be recruited from other social ranks, owing their careers to one or another sponsor. Together they are the oligarchs. They specialize in the political realm.

The political realm consumes resources, but it does not produce them. It draws resources from the wellsprings of production, from the labor of common people – but this is what the rich as individuals and families do, too. The two avenues of living off the fruits of labor must run parallel to each other. In societies of agrarian exploitation the flows of rent, tribute, and taxes must be mutually compatible. In a capitalist economy the profits of business and taxation must arrange a harmonious carving of the take. The political realm works these things out with the rich. If it does not, they mobilize forces to subdue a threat of taking "too much" of their income.

At the base of the political realm are the institutions of force: the army, police and all the sheriffs, marshals, government spies, and various special units. When disobedience breaks out here or there, the state rushes force to the scene and teaches a lesson.

The bedrock use of force, and the most important effect of the existence of organs of legal violence, is to maintain the basic economic rules over labor and its output. In ordinary times the state provides this service to the rich, since they are the beneficiaries of the economic order.

The Aristotle we are not taught

It is hardly possible to separate political from economic power. This is not just a matter of corruption of individuals, nor is it only the element of truth in the saying, "You can't beat City Hall," not to mention the bribes and similar methods used to grab lucrative contracts from the government. The political realm can only be understood as a consequence and servant of the fundamental economic relations of a society.

You do not need to be a cynic or a radical to see that the central question of political power is the rich versus the common people. Aristotle, the Greek philosopher and researcher honored in universities for generations, said it 2,500 years ago. Blunt statements abound in his book, *Politics*.

"In a democracy the poor have more power than the rich, because there are more of them, and the will of the majority is supreme."[74]

This statement by itself is ambiguous about which is the essential characteristic for classifying who rules – their economic position or their numbers in a city-state. Aristotle's book as a whole is clear:

"The form of government is a democracy when the free, who are also poor and the majority, govern, and an oligarchy when the rich and the noble govern, they being at the same time few in number."[75]

"For the real difference between democracy and oligarchy is poverty and wealth. Wherever men rule by reason of their wealth, whether they be few or many, that is an oligarchy, and where the poor rule, that is a democracy. But as a fact the rich are few and the poor many."[76]

How often are we told that democracy is about taking votes and doing what the majority wants, with due respect for the minority? Aristotle almost laughs at that definition. True, he divides governments into three categories based on whether political power is held by one man, a few men (and in his time it was all men, no women), or the many. But the real difference is whether the rich or the poor rule, since "as a fact" the rich are few and the poor are the majority. Democracy, a form of rule by the many in the formal classification, is essentially rule by the common people.

By the poor Aristotle refers to the common people, including the working middle layers. He is not talking only about people who fall below a poverty line. (His book attempts one brief exception, discussed below.) Those poor plus the middle make up the common people, the great majority who work or suffer for lack of work. In Aristotle's day the rich despised productive labor and those who did it. The rich thought of themselves as the only genuine human beings, regarding those who worked as little better than animals.

There is a huge gap between the income of the rich and the incomes of the poor and middle, but people in the middle are spread across a range of incomes. This reality is often used to foster paralyzing divisions among them. It is like rivalry on a block to keep the nicest lawn while a mansion in the hills enjoys lush acres maintained by servants. Nonetheless, the incomes of all common people were (and remain) in stark contrast to the incomes of the rich.

Aristotle soon makes it clear that democracy is not merely about who has a vote. The crucial issue is who exercises power in the political realm. He has no fantasy that those in power conduct a poll and then act accordingly. Abraham Lincoln, taking the language of a Bible champion, agreed when he said the goal is not merely government for the people, but government *by* the people.

(This distinction should not be confused with the fact that every social group must have political agents. Not everyone can specialize in governing, simply because most people must concentrate on their economic role. Over time an egalitarian order can steadily broaden the ranks of those who govern, making it part of their working life.)

Aristotle's focus on who exercises power is built into the very structure of the *Politics*. The book is a comparative study of the make-up of states and their constitutions, both 158 actual examples like Sparta and Carthage as well as imagined possibilities and variations. What is a constitution? It is the arrangements of political power. Another English word for the Greek term is "regime." A constitution is not merely a set of laws. When Aristotle speaks of "measures which are really destructive to the laws or to the constitution," he implies that a constitution is more than laws, even a document of basic laws.[77] He remarks about an essay by Plato, "In the *Laws* there is hardly anything but laws; not much is said about the constitution."[78]

Aristotle maintains that "a constitution is the arrangement of magistracies (officials) in a state, especially of the highest of all. ... The constitution is in fact the government. For example, in democracies the people are supreme, but in oligarchies, the few; and, therefore, we say that these two forms of government also are different, and similarly in other cases."[79]

The constitution, Aristotle teaches, is the set of institutions from which certain people exercise fundamental power. The issue is about who has power to do what, especially to take action or block it on big issues. We typically think of the U.S. Constitution as a written document of basic laws. Yet it is cluttered with provisions like one giving Congress the power to establish post offices and post roads. Very nice. The debate on the constitution in official and academic circles is whether this agreement among the rich of the eighteenth century must be read literally or as a so-called living document. The split on this point is roughly parallel to the difference between conservatives and reformists – let the rich do what they want without government interference, or help the rich in spite of themselves by repairing economic problems that cannot be ignored. It is really a dispute among capitalists, but it cannot be stated in such candid terms in front of the modern public.

Aristotle began from a deeper issue: how do the rich and the common people participate in governing? He lived in an era and a place where common people were aware of their economic interests and eager to participate in politics. They were family farmers; blacksmiths, tanners, and other craftsmen; and small traders. Many of them had time to participate in political life. If there must be democracy, Aristotle hopes common people who are eligible under the constitution to participate in the legislature cannot really afford to do so:

"The best material of democracy is an agricultural population" because "they have no leisure and therefore do not often attend the assembly."[80]

On the other hand, working people in the city "are far inferior ... whether they be mechanics or traders or laborers. ... People of this class can readily come to the assembly because they are continually moving about in the city and in the agora [marketplace]; whereas husbandmen are scattered over the country."[81]

Today, when nearly everyone in middle and lower income ranks must concentrate on holding a job and keeping a family together, it is typical to have formal rule by majority vote while in reality oligarchs run things. One excuse given for this situation is that small cities could be governed by direct democracy of all interested adults, but a modern country with tens of millions of citizens can only have representative legislatures. Most of us can be no more than voters and occasional excited activists.

A little thought refutes such pessimism. One alternative, for example, would be to set aside two hours every two weeks as part of each working person's job that is devoted to participation in government. Also, select a portion of office-holders by random lottery, a widespread practice of ancient Greek cities; this measure is especially effective for citizen audit committees. These are a few ways to practice broad, intense democracy. They would reduce the need for overstuffed bureaucratic staffs and career elected officials, two anti-democratic burdens that make government suffocating to the average person. Population size poses a minor problem for the practice of democracy, and it is not difficult to solve. The big issue is who rules, the rich or the common people.

Aristotle could not yearn to be modern, but he and the oligarchs of today agree on excluding common people from the regime:

"Even if they have no share in office, the poor, provided only that they are not outraged or deprived of their property, will be quiet enough."[82]

The oligarchs' attitude toward common people is clear when Aristotle says, "The beginning of reform is not so much to equalize property [among the rich, as was done in Sparta] as to train the nobler sort of natures not to desire more, and to prevent the lower from getting more; that is to say, they must be kept down, but not ill-treated."[83] Aristotle also made blunt statements about the need to avoid serious change.

"Friendship [among members of the ruling class] we believe to be the greatest good of states and the preservative of them against revolutions."

"We should be able further to say how a state may be constituted under any given conditions; both how it is originally formed and, when formed, how it may be longest preserved."[84]

Why should a state always be preserved? Aristotle has a scientist's interest to "ascertain the modes of ruin and preservation ... of constitutions,"[85] but he studies the subject in order to keep a regime going. He never considers whether a regime has become rotten and deserves to go, let alone whether a political power can be the instrument of building a new economic order. Rather:

"In the opinion of some, the regulation of property is the chief point of all [state constitutions], that being the question upon which all revolutions turn."[86]

The books of Aristotle that have come down to us are notes of lectures delivered in his school, the Lyceum, or summaries written by the lecturer for the library. He was not the only instructor, but the books are in his name. Altogether there are several sources of variation in the body of work attributed to Aristotle, even within the lecture series on politics.

For the most part, the *Politics* draws a sharp line between the rich and the rest. There is one section, however, where the book places hope in a large middle class distinct from both rich and poor.

"Now in all states there are three elements: one class is very rich, another very poor, and a third in a mean."

"But a city ought to be composed, as far as possible, of equals and similars; and these are generally the middle classes."

"Those states are likely to be well-administered in which the middle class is large, and stronger if possible than both the other classes."

"Great then is the good fortune of a state in which the citizens have a moderate and sufficient property; for where some possess much, and the others nothing, there may arise an extreme democracy, or a pure oligarchy; or a tyranny may grow out of either extreme – either out of the most rampant democracy, or out of an oligarchy; but it is not so likely to arise out of the middle constitutions."[87]

Even this section of the *Politics* proceeds from the ground that a political arrangement reflects economic divisions. Aristotle does not regard major economic change as a political task. After all, that is a revolutionary program, but he and his associates were interested in preventing revolutions.

The above passages, concentrated within a few pages of each other, end with a realistic admission that the whole discussion was an academic aside:

"Most governments are either democratical or oligarchical. The reason is that the middle class is seldom numerous in them, and whichever party, whether the rich or the common people, transgresses the mean and predominates, draws the constitution its own way, and thus arises either oligarchy or democracy."[88]

In fact, ancient democracy like the one in Athens was rule by the common people, what we today would call the middle class and the poor as one group. They restricted but did not eliminate the rich. Common people had the upper hand in running the political realm. This is different than voting on questions and persons offered by oligarchs. However, the common people could not use their political power to abolish the rich as economic beings. The foundations did not exist for an egalitarian economic order. Today the productive power of humanity has developed to the point that a new commonwealth is possible. In fact, it is the only way to throw off our growing burden of economic oppressions.

Athenian democracy was a historical rarity in what began as one of the small city-states dotting the mountain-divided lands of Greece. Although most working people were poor and middle income farmers, the slaves at the silver mines of Laurium provided much of the public wealth that gave craftsmen, shop owners, and some peasants time to run the political realm. The state paid needy citizens a subsidy for each day they were on official business. This arrangement came to undermine their economic role.

The Athenian state hemmed in the rich, and the irreconcilable clash of interest between the rich and common people was displaced to an outward push. Athens acquired an empire. That set in motion a dynamic that rotted out the foundations of democracy. First the Macedonians under Philip II and his son Alexander (tutored by Aristotle!), then the Romans, subjugated Athens and its colonies to a wider empire of the rich.

For all the honor paid to Aristotle today, the class realities that he explained to his students are buried under piles of commentary. Aristotle's father was doctor to a king, and Aristotle himself had a number of household servants or slaves. He taught the sons of the rich. His aim was to understand the forms of political rule in the era of agrarian exploitation. With that understanding he could recommend stable institutions for the rich. Our aim must be to understand the political realm in order to get rid of the economic order based on industrial labor and proceed to a new commonwealth.

Demolishing the oligarchs' political realm

The lesson from Aristotle's time and plenty of history since then is that it is impossible to change the existing economic order into an egalitarian economy by passing laws. Nor can we change the essential character of the political realm by replacing oligarchs with our leaders in the same offices. There is no way to make the oligarchy agree to change its spots, pass legislation that enacts the no rich, no poor program, and enforce it, all with the blessing of judges trained and selected for devotion to the existing regime.

Such dreams smudge the fundamental difference between adjustments in the existing economic order and reconstruction that makes a new commonwealth. The job is to overturn the oligarchic regime, breaking its institutions into pieces and replacing them with our own, staffed by individuals of proven dedication to the no rich, no poor program. Common people need their own political regime. The Declaration of Independence said the same thing in 1776:

"Whenever any form of government becomes destructive of these ends, it is the right of the people to alter or to abolish it, and to institute new government, laying its foundation on such principles and organizing its powers in such form, as to them shall seem most likely to effect their safety and happiness. Prudence, indeed, will dictate that governments long established should not be changed for light and transient causes; and accordingly all experience has shown that mankind is more disposed to suffer while evils are sufferable than to right themselves by abolishing the forms to which they are accustomed. But when a long train of abuses and usurpations pursuing invariably the same object evinces a design to reduce them under absolute despotism, it is their right, it is their duty, to throw off such government, and to provide new guards for their future security."

The Declaration talks about rights and duty, but it also summarizes social experience. A regime and the few whom it serves must become outrageous before people will rise up, break it apart, and institute a new power and social order. The regime must cross a certain line in its violations of accepted understandings of what common people shall have and what oligarchs shall not take.

The tipping point is not the worst oppression and poverty ever recorded. Indeed, people can see that vast improvement in our lives is at hand, but an obdurate regime blocks it. When the

134

choice is to lose one's station in life or to join together and toss aside an arbitrary oligarchy, then the time of regime change is near.

It is easy to feel hopeless today. A fundamental upheaval in the United States seems infinitely far off, blocked by the screaming of the media; the advice, warnings and threats of reformist leaders; and repression in reserve. Can common people demolish the regime of the rich and replace it with one committed to the principles of no rich and no poor, full employment, and corporations of economic service?

Yes. A study of fundamental change shows that it occurs when three conditions are met. We can learn from previous revolutions whether or not we like the programs they implemented at their moments in history.

The first condition exists when the current regime becomes extremely narrow. It serves only a few thieves who plunder the whole economy, pushing everyone else into a corner. The French Revolution of 1789 overthrew the decadent regime of Louis the 16th and well-connected aristocrats around him. The Russian Revolution of 1917 chased out the czar, who was utterly out of touch with the common people of his country. The Chinese revolution of 1925-1949 defeated Chiang Kai-shek and four super-rich families who took whatever caught their eye from hundreds of millions of people. A revolution in Iran in 1977-79 drove out the Shah and the circle of state-sponsored thieves around him.

135

The ruling circles of the United States are well on the way to such open plunder. In September 2008 the secretary of the treasury, who came from the investment banking gang of Goldman Sachs, demanded that Congress give him $700 billion of "bailout" money, what turned out to be only a first installment, with no strings attached and almost no provision for reviewing the disbursement of the funds. After one vote bowing to a flood of constituent protest, Congress appropriated the funds. Every month since then, even under a new president and a new treasury secretary, new examples of greed and corruption in the bailout have come to light.

The ordinary workings of the financial establishment display similar looting. A hundred years ago J.P. Morgan was a wealthy, immensely powerful banker. He grabbed plenty for himself. Still, he maintained a connection with economic development, putting railroads and the steel industry back on their feet in monopolies after experience showed that free-market competition ruined everyone. Wall Street today cannot point to any similar industrial revival. Hedge funds and private buyout firms take over corporations only to break union contracts, raid the pension fund, lay off a chunk of the staff and double the workload of the rest, then sell the remains to the next wheeler-dealer.

Chief executives run corporations into the ground, then retire with tens and hundreds of millions of dollars.

A lone operator named Bernie Madoff piled up a $70 billion Ponzi scheme over two decades. Giant Wall Street firms saw that he was a fraud and stayed away from him, but they did not blow the whistle. The federal Securities and Exchange Commission, presented with unmistakable warnings, refused to investigate. A reporter for the Wall Street Journal was too busy enjoying a lucrative career to follow up story leads that were as loud as a jackhammer.

The second condition of basic change is in place when wide sections of the people are ready to see the existing order go away. The world view of the old order crumbles, and the outline of a new order comes into view. A corrosive, liberating Enlightenment preceded the French Revolution. During the twenty years before two Russian revolutions in 1917, industrial workers forged a deep commitment to socialism. In China people knew for a hundred years that imperial dynasties could not cope with the modern world; they looked at several different Western ideological offerings one after another, ending up with a homegrown transformation of Marxism. Much ferment preceded the Iranian revolution, too. Some of it was left-wing, but an Islamic doctrine preached for many years by the ayatollah Khomeini turned out to be dominant. Regardless of what we think about these ideas, they show that big change is built on a widespread turning away from the existing order toward something new.

It appears that the United States is at the beginning of this process. As these lines are written, the oligarchic regime is cleaning up appearances with the ground-breaking selection of Barack Obama to replace the most despised president in modern U.S. history. Right in the middle of the 2008 election, though, the silent grinding down of common people turned into a turbulent era of financial shock, a deep recession, and growing antagonism between the United States and other big economic powers.

The third condition is a definite program for a new order and an organization of people committed to fight for it and implement it. They are only a tiny percentage of the population, but such an organization is the lever with which common people topple the oligarchs, put together immediate relief for the masses, organize the inevitable battles of self-defense, and start building the new order.[89]

When these conditions mature, seemingly solid institutions crack, depriving an isolated, despised oligarchy of reliable instruments of power.

We may learn by comparing the approaching birth of a new commonwealth with the run-up to the Civil War of 1861-65. From as early as the Missouri Compromise of 1820, the Northern majority tried to work out a side-by-side accommodation with the plantation South. Their diverging economic interests did not allow it. Instead, the confrontation grew wider and became irreconcilable. By 1861 the northern economy of farmers, industrialists, and workers could no longer give in to Southern geographic expansionism, which ripened to outright secession as part of a claim to most of the continent for slavery.

A bedrock labor matter moved with lumbering but irresistible force to the center of social issues and politics. The current economic dilemma of common people will do the same.

However, the Civil War was a massive shedding of blood because it was a clash of two lands within one country. The South had not entered an internal crisis. The plantation owners had the rest of Southern society under control. Two entire societies faced each other. Today, the overwhelming majority of one population is separating itself from a narrow oligarchy that rules for the rich and only the rich. The clash of interests is as fundamental as in the Civil War, but the climactic historical moment will reflect the latent strength of the common people.

It is invaluable to know where things are going based on the history of labor as sketched in this essay. In the here and now, the main thing is the program.

It won't happen without a program

One of the most important questions to ask anyone who offers political advice is, what is your program?

If someone advocates a reform, they want action, and that is the only way things change. Still, what program is advocated? If someone shuts the door on everything except a certain package of reforms, arguing that nothing more is needed or achievable, that amounts to accepting the continued erosion of living conditions.

Several days after the 2008 election of Barack Obama as president, activist Dan La Botz advocated something like a program. It is a good example of many similar statements, sincere and heartfelt. Before he got to the details, La Botz noted that many of Obama's volunteer campaigners were ambitious persons seeking a job in the new administration or a piece of the largesse it might hand out to states and cities. In a country of more than 300 million people, the candidate's organization – hip, efficient, and well-financed with startup money from hedge fund moguls and the like – broke new ground by recruiting perhaps a million volunteers.

La Botz wrote:

"The future lies in the struggle for all of the implicit agendas wrapped up in those hopes [placed in an Obama presidency]:

To end the wars in Iraq and Afghanistan now and leave not one base, not one soldier behind.

To provide jobs for all and leave not one person unemployed.

To win labor union representation and living wages.

To bring a national health care system to all Americans.

To protect pensions and strengthen social security so that all retire in comfort and dignity.

To insure not one home lost, not one person homeless.

Having seen the presidential racial barrier broken, to bring racial justice to all Americans.

To end poverty, and to stop the process which produces it.

To gain GLBT rights, including the right to marry.

To win rights for immigrants now."[90]

Most of these agendas, as La Botz calls them, are excellent goals. Few people would disagree with more than one or two of them. The list even includes an element of the no rich, no poor program. Events might bring one or another item to the center of mass political involvement. That's beyond our power to determine; when it happens, let's join the action. However, the next move will not be to bring in nine additional agendas. No movement can juggle so many loosely joined concerns.

The real problem is that the list is not a program. La Botz almost surely has a vision behind his agendas. We can make a good guess about it by enlarging his reforms. He wants the United States to live at peace with the world, bringing an end to wars that have drained our resources and maimed so much innocent flesh, from Korea in the 1950s to Vietnam in the 1960s

141

to Afghanistan today. He wants an economy that has some rich persons but no poor people. He wants the same harmony regardless of cultural individualities that Rodney King asked for: "Can we all get along?"

Like any serious thinker La Botz has a vision of a good society. All the same, neither a list of reforms nor a vision takes the place of a program. A program goes directly at a social order. It demands certain basic principles of operation for society.

A program states or clearly implies who will gain and who will lose. The program for a new commonwealth will benefit all common people while costing the rich their riches. Later, things will be better for everyone in the society, but a solution that evades the conflict is no solution at all.

It takes a big social upheaval to put a major program into effect, defend it from inevitable attack, and consolidate it so that the new commonwealth lasts. The first advocates cannot go out and recruit a mass movement. History, it seems, obeys a speed limit for decades – then it puts the pedal to the floor, and everything happens in a flash. Most of the time we don't know where we are in this journey.

Advocates of a new society cannot substitute for millions of common people. They will pour into the streets when they are ready. Too often activists go beyond testing whether a mass action is possible. They convince themselves that they can (really: must) build a movement. Acknowledging the necessity of starting where people are, they put aside any real program, telling themselves and whoever will listen that a reformist scheme will speed up history.

People committed to an egalitarian society can take the no rich, no poor program into all corners of society, adapting to the ebb and flow of events. "The hollow sound of 'equal opportunity' must die away, and the call for equality sounded across the land."[91]

At some point common people will organize around their program. If they form a New Commonwealth party, it will be like any third party – yet different. It will campaign for reforms that benefit common people and against "reforms" that oppress them. If the party is able to elect representatives, they take the political struggle into Congress, but it would be an illusion to think that some day a majority of legislators will enact the no rich, no poor program under the regime of the oligarchs.

Typically, a third party finds that one of the two major parties takes over much of its program. This is not surprising, because the program aims to modify the existing economic order, not replace it. Along the way the two major parties sometimes break up and regroup. Realignment has happened several times in the United States, where the political system is built on having exactly two big parties. Both parties have been two things at once: instruments of the rich and coalitions of numerous secondary economic interest groups. If there were only one party, there would be no safety valve for discontent. The writers of the Constitution, especially James Madison, designed the U.S. political system to frustrate expression of the common interest of all common people.[92]

A New Commonwealth party begins in the existing regime, but it is an agent for a new order. When days of decision arrive, the crucial questions will be these: Do the common people want the existing order to go? Is there an organized core of dedicated fighters for the no rich, no poor program? If so, the country can sweep aside the oligarchs and bring the New Commonwealth into being. Otherwise, the old order will beat back the challenge. People will need time to recuperate, ponder again what program will solve their problems, and gather new determination. History will go through the cycle again, hardly seeming to move for years and then arriving at a moment of truth. During the slow years, the key question is, what is your program?

The crash and recession of 2008

Since 1973 most people in the United States have worked longer hours than their parents. Their hourly pay lagged the growth of production, stretching inequality of income to a historical extreme. Retirement security became like a mirage, always hovering over the next dune. Maintaining health care for the family and education for the children became major projects.

Looking back, the denial of hopes is clear, but the losses were like an advancing glacier, moving a few inches year after year.

One temporary way to cope with the squeeze was to take on debt. From about the mid-1990s, banks offered people cheap credit: no-down low-interest mortgages, home equity loans, a new charge card in the mail almost every week, student loans and more. Common people took on debt because they were not getting solid pay increases while the cost of housing, a health plan, and other essentials kept going up. Banks in league with mortgage brokers and Wall Street firms wrote $35 billion of fantasy subprime home mortgages in 1994, $200 billion annually in the first few years of the 21st century, and $625 billion in the peak year of 2005.[93]

The barrier to mass prosperity under capitalism became more apparent. Although investment money went into high technology, it did not create a socially significant number of good jobs. A few people were winners in electronics, software, the Internet, and biotechnology, but the leading industries were not mass job creators like the automobile industry in its glory days.

The big practitioners of financial gymnastics were hedge funds and other private capital groups. They were good at grabbing profit out of the economy. Mass prosperity was absent while

145

the rich enjoyed several asset booms in hi-tech stocks, dot-com fantasies, and securitized mortgages.[94]

It could not last. When the crash arrived in September-October 2008, it was historic in the gloomiest sense of the word. It unleashed a downturn that threatens to match the enormity of the depression of the 1930s.

A depression is politically dangerous to the oligarchs. Unemployment jumps and consumption drops. These things do not happen because crops failed or factories were bombed. A depression testifies that the economic relationships in a society have escaped human control – or they are rigged in favor of the rich with no concern for how much suffering they cause common people. Either way, a depression silently makes the case for changing our economic institutions. It creates a political opening for a fundamental program that will do just that.

In 2008 the financial crisis included a bust in housing and other real estate prices, mind-boggling government handouts to the largest banks and Wall Street operators and the failure of one of them (Lehman Brothers), a stock market plunge, and finally the revelation in December that a recession of the whole economy had begun a year earlier. The crash was called financial because it hit the prices of a thousand different forms of financial paper. This stuff consists of claims to money expected or promised at future moments. There are stocks, which claim dividends and the proceeds if a business is sold (stock prices may also enjoy an approximate rise in step with nominal corporate profits); bonds, which are promises to pay regular interest and a repayment of initial principal; and insurance policies, which take regular premium payments on one side, promising a coverage amount if a specified event occurs on the other side. Innumerable combinations are built on top of these contracts.

A global house of cards collapsed. Such crashes have happened many times before in the history of capitalism, but no two are the same. This time around, tens of millions of working and retired people saw the security and comfort of their retirement disappear. The reason is employers' widespread use of defined contribution retirement accounts. We saw earlier how retirement security has eroded since the mid-1970s.

The crash of 2008 showed how little both conservatives and reformists have to offer.

Conservatives responded two ways. A few of them stuck to their ideology, insisting that market events should be left to unfold on their own. The conservatives with power, however, turned to the federal government and the governments of other countries. Treasury Secretary Henry Paulson, previously an executive at investment bank Goldman Sachs, gave money to Wall Street firms that are "too big to fail." That action rescued some threatened retirement paper, such as annuities issued by the AIG firm, which received $123 billion of aid and loans in two fat handouts.[95] Some action was necessary to prevent even more carnage of financial paper that constitutes the money existence of tens of millions of people, of cities and counties, and banks that finance the daily operations of businesses.

However, as soon as the financial crash revealed itself to be the opening stage of a general economic downturn, conservatives insisted that common people must bear the burden. When big banks got hundreds of billions of dollars each, the money was shoveled to them with hardly a second glance. When Detroit automobile corporations said they could not survive without several tens of billions of dollars, conservative oligarchs stood in the doorway, demanding that auto workers take impoverishing cuts in pay as well as in benefits they had obtained by giving up wage increases year after year. Congress also extorted a no-strike clause from their union. Of course, the auto workers' wages (exaggerated in the press at $70 an hour but actually $28 an hour on average, only $14 for new hires) had nothing to do with flaky mortgages, fancy credit swap trading, and all the other outrages of Wall Street. In round two of the auto industry carnage, Washington demanded still more sacrifice from auto workers.

So much for conservative ideology.

Reformists responded to the crash by rummaging through the closet for more sophisticated government measures. Buy stock in banks; nationalize them; launch public works projects in a big way; extend unemployment insurance; buy mortgages; rewrite mortgages through banks or directly with homeowners; send one-time checks to every income taxpayer; raise the income tax rate on the rich; and on and on.

Many of the proposals are fine ideas and could do what they promise. However, they are all about helping the economic system get through the crunch. The reformists did almost nothing to oppose the economic order.

The no rich, no poor program will double Social Security benefits. The reformists cannot do that, because it demands too much from the rich. The no rich, no poor program will reconstitute society on a foundation of guaranteeing full employment and leveling up people to equality and mass prosperity. Reformists cannot imagine such a thing. The no rich, no poor program will turn corporations into enterprises competing to supply needed products on a breakeven basis, not profit. Incidentally, this change can do away with 99 percent of the Wall Street paper that was the stuff of the financial collapse.

Reformists spin elaborate policy proposals at best. They no longer have a challenging criticism of capitalism and hence no solid program. Reformists as a political trend have proved again and again that common people must turn elsewhere for an end to the growing economic nightmare.

149

During the 1930s millions of people questioned why we should stick with capitalism, but it survived, delivering gains in the 1950s and 1960s. Hopefully, the current downturn will not match the great depression of the 1930s. There will be a recovery of some sort, but it will not begin a period of happy days. The erosion since 1973 of secure jobs, health care, and retirement; of educational opportunity; of public facilities and clean, safe communities – the denial of the good life that should be ours in the 21st century – is now a permanent feature of the existing economic order. Common people are just going have to say enough is enough, take things over, and guarantee prosperity for all in a New Commonwealth. We will all have work to do, and we will all sit down to feast at the same table.

Appendix

If we took all the personal income in 2007 and paid it equally to everyone who wanted a job, each of us would earn $72,394 a year for a full-time position.

The calculation is presented in the accompanying table. We use government economic statistics to see how big the pie is and how many people would divide it up. Our methods ensure that the estimate is a conservative one.[96]

The major ingredient of the pie is personal consumption expenditures, which is less than personal income. We use it in order to get closer to an estimate of how much "real stuff" each of us could have. By beginning with consumption expenditures, we also remove the mirage of paper profits that were booked and distributed as income but later written off without ever being spent on goods or services. However, we want to count pre-tax income, so we add personal current taxes paid, which is primarily income taxes plus contributions to Social Security and the like.

Equal wage computation for 2007		
Personal consumption expenditures	9,710	
Personal current taxes (income tax, not sales tax)	1,493	
Federal social insurance receipts		870
Employee social insurance contributions - assume 50%	435	
Trade deficit	708	
Social security payout	595	
Beneficiaries (retired, spouses, children, disabled) (000)		49,865
Average monthly benefit		987
Target multiple of Social Security		2
Remainder to be financed	595	
Employed (000)		146,047
Average work week (hours)		39.1
Implied FT person-years (000)	142,761	
The calculation		
Personal consumption + personal current taxes + social insurance contributions	11,638	
Subtract trade deficit and expansion of Social Security	10,335	
Equal wage	$72,394	

Again being conservative, we subtract the trade deficit, the excess of imports over exports, so that we get closer to counting goods and services we produce. We also subtract the funds needed to double Social Security benefits for retirees and disabled people.

Our goal is to spread the pie equally among all jobs, so we take the number of full-time jobs in the country. This figure is calculated from the average number of people employed on any day during the year, then converting to a full-time equivalent by using the average length of their work week.

Division of the income pie by the number of jobs gives the result: $72,425 a year.

The calculation is inevitably "what if." What if more people wanted to work, and part-time workers wanted full-time jobs? On one hand, that would require more income and more production of the things people would buy – but of course, more working hours means more production.

No one expects to divide the fruits of our labor equally next year. The calculation of the equality wage provides a point for comparing who gets less and who takes more. This essay explores changes in the nature and the social relations of work. The starting point is the enormous inequality of income today. "What if" leads to "Why not?"

The calculation is for the year 2007, before the crash of 2008. It registers what our economy

153

showed we could do before the financial crisis. That collapse did not suddenly make us less capable of producing things. The same machines still exist. The same people are available to work. The forced idleness of millions of laid-off employees took its toll, as did the shutdown or contraction of businesses that could not get credit or find customers. Today we can produce as much, even more, than we did in 2007.

Notes

[1] Bureau of Labor Statistics, "Employee Tenure In The Mid-1990s," news release, January 30, 1997; Bureau of Labor Statistics, "Employee Tenure In 2006," news release, Sept. 8, 2006. The starting year in this report is 1983. For women the percentage with ten-year tenure has moved up and down; it was 28 percent as of 2006.

[2] U.S. Census, *Income, Poverty, and Health Insurance Coverage in the United States: 2007*, Table A-2, at www.census.gov/prod/2008pubs/p60-235.pdf; John Schmitt, *Unions and Upward Mobility for Young Workers*, Washington, DC, Center for Economic and Policy Research, Oct. 2008, p. 2 and Fig. 1.

[3] U.S. Bureau of Labor Statistics, *Employment & Earnings*, January 2008, 55:1, Table A24; Philip L. Rones et al, "Trends in hours of work since the mid-1970s," *Monthly Labor Review*, April 1997, Table 2.

[4] The median income for people age 50 to 54 runs around 16 to 19 percent greater than the income for people age 30 to 34, with a gradual rise over the years in between. U.S. Census Bureau, *Current Population Survey: 2007 Annual Social and Economic Supplement*, Table PINC-01, at pubdb3.census.gov/macro/032007/perinc/new01_001.htm and U.S. Census Bureau, *Current Population Survey: 2008 Annual Social and Economic Supplement*, Table PINC-01, at pubdb3.census.gov/macro/032008/perinc/new01_055.htm. People who reach $72,000 in their early fifties typically spent decades below the equality line.

[5] Among people who worked full-time year-round in 2007, 19.5 percent had income of $72,500 or more. This is all their money income, not only their job earnings. Millions more worked part-time, and among all those who worked during the year, the rich were 15 percent. U.S. Census Bureau, *Current Population Survey: 2008 Annual Social and Economic Supplement*, Table PINC-01, at pubdb3.census.gov/macro/032008/perinc/new01_055.htm. Of course, most part-time workers did not earn the $35 per hour that corresponds to $72,500 a year. As discussed in the text, few of those who get over $72,000 in a particular year, especially if their earnings are still under about $100,000 a year, earn that amount (adjusted for inflation) throughout their working life. Well over 90 percent of the population would gain if everyone who wanted an income had a job, and that job paid $72,000 a year in 2007 dollars.

[6] U.S. Census Bureau, *Current Population Survey, 2008 Annual Social and Economic Supplement*, Table PINC-05, at pubdb3.census.gov/macro/032008/perinc/new05_001.htm.

[7] To be sure, inequality of salaries and wages is big, too. The median earnings for full-time workers was $40,320, meaning half the employees earned less than that amount and half earned more. The gap between the median and the average of $51,556 speaks to the inequality of wages, ignoring all other sources of income.

[8] Simon Kuznets, "Long-Term Changes in the National Income of the United States of America Since 1870," in Simon Kuznets, ed., *Income & Wealth of the*

156

United States: Trends and Structure, Cambridge, MA, Bowes & Bowes, pp. 86, 136.

[9] William Beaty, "How Do Transistors Work? No, How Do They Really Work?", 1995, at amasci.com/amateur/transis.html. Lilienfeld received three patents: 1,745,175, Method and Apparatus for Controlling Electric Currents; 1,877,140, Amplifier for Electric Current; and 1,900,018, Device for Controlling Electric Current.

[10] A Thumbnail History of Electronics, at www.ee.umd.edu/~taylor/Electrons8.htm.

[11] What is the difference between biological ancestors of the human species and humans themselves? ""The continuities between chimpanzee tool-behavior and that of humans are clearly traced by Goodall. In this respect, the discontinuities – what chimpanzees cannot do – assume particular importance in accurately identifying the unique character of human labor activity." (Charles Woolfson, *The Labour Theory of Culture*, London, Routledge and Kegan Paul, 1982, p. 38) Biological evolution produced something new that broke free of biological evolution: a species living by labor, which develops in its own ways rather than by physiological change.

[12] Changes in work now cause small changes in the body. For example, when there is a rapid change from eating mostly meat to a diet of cooked grains and vegetables, the jaw muscles shrink. However, teeth do not evolve as quickly, and the result is dental problems. About 2,300 years ago a wave of people called the Yayoi moved from what is now Korea and China into Japan, settling among the Jomon hunting people. The Yayoi brought rice-based agriculture.

157

They intermarried with the Jomon. Today, a number of Japanese people have noticeably crowded and crooked teeth. Hillary Mayell, "Evolving to Eat Mush: How Meat Changed Our Bodies," *National Geographic News*, February 18, 2005.

[13] See Mark Nathan Cohen, *The Food Crisis in Prehistory*, New Haven, Yale University Press, 1977.

[14] "Peasant families control a given set of lands at any one time, cultivate it, rely on its produce to survive, and also give a part of the produce to a landlord if they have one, and/or to the state if it exists." (Chris Wickham, *Framing the Early Middle Ages: Europe and the Mediterranean 400-800*, Oxford University Press, 2005, p. 260.)

[15] "They (landowners) do not ... in general control the processes of agrarian production, which tend to remain in the hands of the peasants. ... Peasants determined how their agriculture was going to work, and sought to ensure that their own subsistence was guaranteed first of all." (Wickham, p. 536.)

[16] P. A. Brunt, *Social Conflicts in the Roman Republic*, New York, Norton, 1971, p. 34f.

[17] Neal Wood, *Cicero's Social and Political Thought*, Berkeley, University of California Press, 1988, p. 33.

[18] Shawn Ni and Pham Hoang Van, ""High Corruption Income as a Source of Distortion and Stagnation: Some Evidence from Ming and Qing China," Dec. 2003, pp. 1, 8, 17; prepared for seminar at University of Colorado Denver, at econ.cudenver.edu/home/SeminarPapers/van.pdf.

158

[19] Defenders of material inequality today glorify it in the past. One historian, for example, recognizing an ancient time when "the few tended to become richer, the rest poorer," asserts, "The fact of the matter was that limitations of ancient technology made civilization very costly. Only when many toiled and suffered deprivation could a privileged few have the leisure and ease needful for the creation and maintenance of high culture. ... Such achievements are easily underrated in a democratic age, when men are more likely to sympathize with the slave or serf than with his master." (William H. McNeill, *The Rise of the West*, Chicago, University of Chicago Press, 1991, pp. 287, 661.) Most of the privileged few enjoyed their leisure and ease in political infighting, war, and decadence that did nothing for peasants and other toilers. The agrarian era was an inevitable stage of human life, but the terms of exploitation were variable and could have been much easier on the common people. In the period when agriculture advanced beyond gardening but exploiters had not yet consolidated their rule into so-called civilization, material development and the expansion of society beyond the village were rapid. As soon as agrarian exploiters fastened themselves on the people, progress slowed, sometimes to a millennium of stagnation. The privileged did more to retard productiveness and general well-being than to advance them. Agrarian civilization was a dead weight on the aching backs of the unprivileged many.

[20] Frederic Seebohm, *The English Village Community*, London, Longmans, 1905, esp. pp. 113, 117, 228, 229f., 236, 244, 369. Later scholars have corrected Seebohm's claim that feudal lords imposed

equality on the peasants. Village equality goes back to clan and tribal origins.

21 "New rice seeds included differential ranges of early ripening, late ripening, and drought resistant varieties which allowed for infinite incremental alterations in cropping systems adapted to maximize yields in different soil, drainage and climatic environments – including both inter-regional adjustments and adaptation to relatively small increments in local elevations." In other parts of the country, corn was introduced into wheat-growing areas as a second annual crop. Robert M. Hartwell, "Fifteen Centuries of Chinese Environmental History: Creating a Retroactive Decision-Support System," 1994, at citas.csde.washington.edu/org/report_c.

22 Hill Gates, *China's Motor: A Thousand Years of Petty Capitalism*, Ithaca, Cornell University Press, 1996, p. 48.

23 Even if non-farmers went from 5 to 20 percent of the population while it doubled, most common people remained peasants.

	Before	After
Total	100	200
Peasant	95	160
Non-farming	5	40

24 Yemelyan Pugachev organized an army of 10,000 Cossack peasants in a rebellion to destroy Russian feudalism. His program promised to abolish all "recurring levies, soul tax or other money taxes" and granted peasants "possession of the land, the woods, the hay meadows, the fishing grounds, the salt lakes, without payment or rent, and we free all those peas-

ants and other folk hitherto oppressed by the male-factor gentry and the bribe takers and judges of the towns from the dues and burdens placed upon them." Pugachev saw no need for nobles, advising the peasants to "seize them, punish them, hang them, treat them in the same way as they, having no Christian feeling, oppressed you, the peasants. With the extermination of these enemies, the malefactor gentry, everyone will be able to enjoy a quiet and peaceful life, which will continue for evermore." (Pugachev, decree of July 1774, at www.rusjournal. com/sobornost.html.) Obviously, this agrarian revolutionary had no vision of economic development toward an industrial world.

25 "The early middle ages marked a period of relative aristocratic weakness: in every post-Roman region except Francia and the Levant, aristocracies were both more localized and poorer than they had been under the empire." (Wickham, p. 827.)

26 S. Lilley, *Men, Machines and History*, revised edition, New York, International Publishers, 1965, p. 62.

27 U.S. Dept. of Labor, *Code of Federal Regulations*, Title 41, Sec. 61-250.2, revised July 1, 2002, CFR.

28 U.S. Dept. of Labor, Report on the American Workforce, 2001, p. 106, at www.bls.gov/opub/ rtaw/pdf/rtaw2001.pdf.

29 Report, p. 102.

30 Ibid.

[31] Harry Braverman, *Labor and Monopoly Capital*, New York, Monthly Review Press, 1974, pp. 428f., 434.

[32] Adam Smith, *An Inquiry into the Nature and Causes of the Wealth of Nations*, 5th edition, 1789, Book I, ch. 1, paragraph 3.

[33] Smith, ibid., Book I, ch. 1, paragraph 4.

[34] Andrew Ure, *The Philosophy of Manufactures*, London, Charles Knight, 1835, p. 19.

[35] Ibid., pp, 19-21.

[36] Frederick Winslow Taylor, *The Principles of Scientific Management*, New York, Harper, 1915, p. 25f. Although Taylor refers here to work depending on mechanics, elsewhere he asserted the value of his methods for routinizing virtually any job. "Every single act of every workman can be reduced to a science." (p. 64).

[37] Ibid., p. 104.

[38] Tom Walsh, "Physicians Cite Continuing Problems with Fourth Year of GIC Tiering," *Vital Signs*, Massachusetts Medical Society, April 2009.

[39] Don DeMoro of the Institute for Health and Social Policy developed this analysis.

[40] K.A. Eagle et al, "Closing the Gap Between Science and Practice: The Need for Professional Leadership," *Health Affairs*, March/April 2003, 22:2, pp. 196-201.

[41] From 1977 to 2006 overall cumulative inflation was 360 percent while cumulative college inflation was 810 percent. Calculated from CPI-U from the

Bureau of Labor Statistics and college costs from The College Board, NY as reported in A History of College Inflation, College Money website at www. collegemoney.com/images/News/News_12_4.pdf.

[42] Project on Student Debt, "Quick Facts About Student Debt," at projectonstudentdebt.org/files/File/Debt_Facts_and_Sources.pdf.

[43] The 2007 median income of men with a bachelor's degree (but no higher degree) stands in the same ratio to the median income of all men with income as in 1991. Among women the premium of a bachelor's degree fell from 81 percent in 1991 to 57 percent in 2007. The proportion of women with bachelor's degrees increased, so part of the decline is built into the arithmetic – but the cost of college still rose much faster than general inflation. *U.S. Census Bureau, Current Population Survey*, Table P-16, at www.census.gov/hhes/www/income/histinc/p16.html.

[44] Commission on the Skills of the American Workforce, *America's Choice: high skills or low wages!*, Rochester, NY, National Center on Education and the Economy, 1990, p. 2.

[45] Ibid.

[46] Ibid., pp. 3, 4.

[47] Ibid., p. 7.

[48] It is apparent, for example, that the energy in nuclear bonds can be released in abundant, safe quantities by an oven-size apparatus of palladium and heavy water receiving a modest input of electrical energy. The name "cold fusion" might or might

not be accurate, and the field of electrochemically induced nuclear reactions is at an early stage, similar to where studies of electricity were before Faraday. There is overwhelming evidence of such transformations of energy. See, for example, Pamela A. Mosier-Boss, Stanislaw Szpak et al, "Triple tracks in CR-39 as the result of Pd-D Co-deposition: evidence of energetic neutrons," *Naturwissenschaften*, 2009, 96, pp. 135-142, and Charles G. Beaudette, *Excess Heat: Why Cold Fusion Research Prevailed*, Concord, NH, Oak Grove Press, 2002, full text at http://lenr-canr.org/ acrobat/BeaudetteCexcessheat. pdf.

[49] Lawrence R. Mishel, Jared Bernstein and Sylvia Allegretto, *The State of Working America 2006-07*, Ithaca, NY, Cornell University Press, 2007, Table 1.11, at www.epi.org/datazone/06/inc_by_fifth.xls.

[50] Ibid., Table 1.9.

[51] Ibid., Fig. 1N.

[52] U.S. Dept. of Labor, Private Pension Plan Bulletin Historical Tables, Table E5, at www.dol.gov/ebsa/pdf/privatepensionplanbulletinhistoricaltables.pdf.

[53] Mishel et al., Table 3.17.

[54] Ibid., Table 1.11.

[55] Internal Revenue Service, *Individual Income Tax Returns*, Publication 1304, Tax Year 2006, Table 1.4.

[56] In other words, corporations will no longer collect and allocate most investment funds as they do now. Society can carry out a balanced investment program that funds projects of breakeven firms; see

164

chapters nine and ten of my *From Capitalism to Equality*, Needle Press, 2000.

57 Richard Elkus, *Winner Take All: How Competitiveness Shapes the Fate of Nations*, New York, Basic Books, 2008, pp. 157, 164.

58 Woodrow Wilson, address to The New York City High School Teachers Association, Jan. 9th, 1909, as shown at www.johntaylorgatto.com/fourthpurpose/short.htm.

59 Judith Banister, "Manufacturing employment in China," *Monthly Labor Review*, July 2005, p. 13.

60 Ibid., p. 11.

61 Jon E. Hilsenrath and Rebecca Buckman, "Factory jobs are falling worldwide," *Wall Street Journal*, October 27, 2003, citing a study by economists at Alliance Capital Management.

62 Paul A. Baran, *The Political Economy of Growth*, New York, Monthly Review Press, 1957, p. 181.

63 Ronald Edsforth, *The New Deal: America's Response to the Great Depression*, Malden, MA, Blackwell, 2000, p. 82.

64U.S. Dept. of Veterans Affairs, "GI-BILL History" at www.gibill.va.gov/GI_Bill_Info/history.htm.

65 Ronald E. Kutscher, "Historical trends, 1950-92, and current uncertainties," *Monthly Labor Review*, November 1993, p. 6 and Table 3; U.S. Bureau of Labor Statistics, Table B-1, at ftp://ftp.bls.gov/pub/suppl/empsit.ceseeb1.txt

66 Michael Johnsen, "Importation panel debates open market," *Drug Store News*, Feb 16, 2004.

[67] International Institute for Labour Studies, *World of Work Report 2008: Income Inequalities in the Age of Financial Globalization*, Geneva, International Labour Organization, 2008, p. 2.

[68] Ibid.

[69] Robert Reich, "How Unequal Can America Get Before We Snap?," talk at University of California at Berkeley, April 5, 2005, at 32 minutes, at podcast.berkeley.edu/media/gspp/ucb_reich-snap.mp3.

[70] Ibid., at 1 hr. 3 mins.

[71] Kevin Rudd, "The Global Financial Crisis," *The Monthly*, 42, Feb. 2009 at www.themonthly.com.au/tm/node/1417.

[72] realm
Etymology: Middle English *realme*, from Anglo-French, alteration of Old French *reiame*, from Latin *regimen* control, at www.merriam-webster.com/dictionary/realm

regimen
Etymology: Middle English, from Medieval Latin *regimin-*, *regimen* position of authority, direction, set of rules, from Latin, steering, control, from *regere* to direct, at www.merriam-webster.com/dictionary/regimen.

[73] A. Geoffrey Woodhead, *Thucydides on the Nature of Power*, Cambridge, MA, Harvard University Press, 1970, pp. 104, 107.

[74] Aristotle, *Politics*, translated by Benjamin Jowett, Book Six, chapter 2, 1317b; page/column number is from Greek text as edited by I. Bekker, Berlin, 1831.

[75] Book Four, chapter 4, 1290b.

[76] Book Three, chapter 8, 1279b-1280a.

[77] Book Two, chapter 8, 1268b.

[78] Book Two, chapter 6, 1265a.

[79] Book Three, chapter 6, 1278b.

[80] Book Six, chapter 4, 1318b.

[81] Book Six, chapter 4, 1319a.

[82] Book Four, chapter 13, 1297b.

[83] Book Two, chapter 7, 1267a.

[84] Book Two, chapter 4, 1262b and Book Four, chapter 1, 1288b.

[85] Book Four, chapter 2, 1289b.

[86] Book Two, chapter 7, 1266a.

[87] Book Four, chapter 11, 1295b; Book Four, chapter 11, 1295b; Book Four, chapter 11, 1295b; Book Four, chapter 11, 1295b-1296a.

[88] Book Four, chapter 11, 1295b; we changed the term to "common people."

[89] Ten activists committed to a new commonwealth for every 50,000 residents can rally people during tumultuous days. In 2008 the United States had 252,218,000 people living in 340 metropolitan areas of 100,000 or more people. (U.S. Census dataset, Metropolitan and micropolitan statistical area population and estimated components of change: April 1, 2000 to July 1, 2008 (CBSA-EST2008-alldata) at www.census.gov/popest/metro/files/

2008/CBSA-EST2008-alldata.csv) That implies a core of 50,000 persons.

90 Dan La Botz, "Election of Barack Obama: The People's Victory? Or the Elite's," ZNet, November 9, 2008, at zcommunications.org/znet/viewArticle/19402.

91 Chris Owens, statement as candidate for Congress, March 25, 2006, at www.soapblox.net/myleftwing/showDiary.do?diaryId=6906.

92 Consider a few remarks from Madison's famous Federalist paper number ten:

"The diversity in the faculties of men, from which the rights of property originate, is not less an insuperable obstacle to a uniformity of interests. The protection of these faculties is the first object of government."

"By a faction I understand a number of citizens, whether amounting to a majority or minority of the whole, who are united and actuated by some common impulse of passion, or of interest, adverse to the rights of other citizens, or to the permanent and aggregate interests of the community."

"But the most common and durable source of factions has been the various and unequal distribution of property. Those who hold and those who are without property have ever formed distinct interests in society."

"When a majority is included in a faction, the form of popular government, on the other hand, enables it to sacrifice to its ruling passion or interest both the public good and the rights of other citizens. To secure the public good and private rights against the danger of such a faction, and at the same time to preserve the spirit and the form of popular government, is then the great object to which our inquiries are directed."

"Democracies have ever been spectacles of turbulence and contention; have ever been found incompatible with personal security or the rights of property."

"The majority, having such coexistent passion or interest, must be rendered, by their number and local situation, unable to concert and carry into effect schemes of oppression." (James Madison, Federalist Paper No. 10, originally published November 22, 1787, at www.thirdworldtraveler.com/Democracy/Federalist10_TAR.html.)

Just like Aristotle, Madison sees that power belongs to either the rich or the common people. Like Aristotle he studies how to make sure power stays with the rich. His language is a bit less candid than that of Aristotle, probably because of the printing press and greater literacy in Madison's time compared with ancient Greece.

Madison's theory leads directly to the two-party system in the United States, but there are other ways to frustrate the will of common people. The multiparty systems of Europe carry out the same purpose by a different mechanism. In the U.S. today, however, parties are becoming irrelevant. The oligarchy finds it cannot tolerate any connection with the rest of society, and policy is sold with commercials like detergent.

[93] Edward M. Gramlich, "America's Second Housing Boom," Opportunity and Ownership Project, Urban Institute, Feb. 2007, No. 7, p. 1 at www.urban.org/UploadedPDF/311418_Second_Housing_Boom.p

df; "The Subprime Mortgage Market," *Annual Report 2007*, Federal Reserve Bank of San Francisco, Fig. 1, at www.frbsf.org/publications/federalreserve/annual/2007/subprime.pdf.

[94] From 1994 to 2007 the workforce expanded by 23 million people. The industry breakdown is instructive. Construction added 2.5 million jobs, but manufacturing lost more than 3 million jobs. Health and education in the private sector added 5.5 million jobs – industries that were not developed by daring new investment. Leisure and hospitality along with retail trade – generally low-wage industries – added about 5 million jobs. Despite the focus on financial maneuvering as the way to make fat profits, the financial services industry added only 1.4 million jobs. Put together, this is not a picture of mass prosperity. Job additions calculated from U.S. Bureau of Labor Statistics, Table B-1, at ftp://ftp.bls.gov/pub/suppl/empsit.ceseeb1.txt. Retail trade estimated as half of the trade, transportation, and utilities category.

[95] Actually, AIG's folly, "insuring" gambles made with derivatives, could have been separated from routine annuities, supporting the latter while letting the former go up in smoke.

[96] Personal consumption expenditures: Bureau of Economic Analysis, Table 1.1.5. Gross Domestic Product, 1929-2007.

Personal current taxes: Bureau of Economic Analysis, Table 3.1. Government Current Receipts and Expenditures, 1929-2007.

Federal social insurance receipts: Office of Management and Budget, Fiscal Year 2009, Table 17.1.

Trade deficit: Bureau of Economic Analysis, Table 1.1.5. Gross Domestic Product, 1929-2007.
Social Security payout: Social Security Admin., *Fast Facts & Figures About Social Security*, 2008, p. 3.
Beneficiaries: Ibid., p. 15.
Employed: Census Bureau, Current Population Survey, annual average, accessed via data.bls.gov
Average work week: Bureau of Labor Statistics, Household Data, Table 21 Persons at work in non-agricultural industries by class of worker and usual full- or part-time status, accessed via data.bls.gov.

www.ingramcontent.com/pod-product-compliance
Lightning Source LLC
LaVergne TN
LVHW011233080426
835509LV00005B/477